A CRITICAL INTRODUCTION TO RELIGION
IN THE AMERICAS

# A Critical Introduction to Religion in the Americas

*Bridging the Liberation Theology and Religious Studies Divide*

Michelle A. Gonzalez

NEW YORK UNIVERSITY PRESS
*New York and London*

NEW YORK UNIVERSITY PRESS
New York and London
www.nyupress.org

References to Internet websites (URLs) were accurate at the time of writing.
Neither the author nor New York University Press is responsible for URLs that
may have expired or changed since the manuscript was prepared.

Library of Congress Cataloging-in-Publication Data
Gonzalez, Michelle A.
A critical introduction to religion in the Americas : bridging the liberation theology
and religious studies divide / Michelle A. Gonzalez.
pages cm    Includes bibliographical references and index.
ISBN 978-1-4798-5306-9 (cloth : alk. paper) — ISBN 978-1-4798-0097-1 (pbk. : alk. paper)
1. Liberation theology—America. 2. African Americans—Religion. 3. Blacks—Religion.
4. Hispanic Americans—Religion. 5. Latin Americans—Religion. I. Title.
BT83.57.G655    2014
230'.0464098—dc23        2014004215

New York University Press books are printed on acid-free paper,
and their binding materials are chosen for strength and durability.
We strive to use environmentally responsible suppliers and materials
to the greatest extent possible in publishing our books.

Manufactured in the United States of America

10 9 8 7 6 5 4 3 2 1

Also available as an ebook

# CONTENTS

## ACKNOWLEDGMENTS

As I look back at my intellectual autobiography, I become aware that the questions that fueled this book first emerged when I was an undergraduate at Georgetown University. Sitting in Diana Hayes's black liberation theology class my senior year, I was challenged not only by the writings of black theologians but also by the way in which I, a Cuban American, identified with so many of their works. That same year I sat in Chester Gillis's feminist theology seminar and felt a similar challenge from feminism as a global religious movement. I must thank these former professors for stimulating ideas in a twenty-year-old that twenty years later I continue to find provocative.

After Georgetown University I went to study in the cradle of U.S. liberation theology, Union Theological Seminary, and was mentored by James H. Cone. In his classes I deepened my knowledge of black liberation theology and was exposed to the diversity of liberation theologies in the United States and throughout the global South. During this time I met the late Cuban American ethicist Ada María Isasi-Díaz. Ada María was not only a mentor but also a dear friend. Her legacy lives on in the many students and colleagues she inspired and befriended throughout the years.

My Ph.D. mentor, Alejandro García-Rivera, also is no longer with us. Alex was always nervous about the reduction of theology to ethics within liberation theologies, and through his research and classes I came to appreciate the significance of the aesthetic for justice. My first academic teaching position at Loyola Marymount University provided the venue for meeting my dear friend and colleague Anthea Butler. Anthea introduced me to the world of lived religion, to scholars who approached the everyday faith of everyday people through the lens of history and ethnography.

After my time at Loyola Marymount but before taking up my current position at the University of Miami, I spent two years as a theologian-in-residence at the Roman Catholic Mission in San Lucas Tolimán, Guatemala. Through collaborating with the late Father Greg Schaffer there, I learned that academic proclamations about the death of liberation theology were untrue. Yet I also learned that the religion of everyday Christians was quite different from the religion described in the pages of academic liberation theology.

My colleagues at the University of Miami continue to foster a very supportive environment for my teaching and research. I want to thank in particular my colleagues Dexter Callender, William Scott Green, and Aman De Sondy for our lengthy conversations about the state of the field of religion, but more important for their friendship and encouragement of my work. I want to thank Jennifer Hammer at New York University Press for giving me the pleasure of working with her again on a book. The three main men in my life—my husband, Byron, and my sons, Byron Manuel and Michael—patiently and compassionately have watched me complete this work.

In the past year, as I have completed this book, we have lost three great figures that are foundational voices in liberation theology: Ada María Isasi-Díaz, Father Greg Schaffer, and Otto Maduro. The three embody liberation theology's pastoral, prophetic, and intellectual contributions. They were my friends, my mentors, our elders. I thank them for taking me under their wing. In this year of mourning their passing, I am constantly comforted by the image of the God of Life so many liberation theologians embrace, a vision that reminds us that death is not the end. In the words of Ada, "La lucha (the struggle) continues."

# Introduction

I discovered the discipline of theology through the writings of liberation theologians. Some would call this a backward approach, yet it is the
one that my education coincidentally and thankfully bestowed on me. I
studied the hermeneutics of suspicion—that is, the examination of texts
with a critical eye—and the need to listen to the voices that emerge from
the underside of history before learning about the normative theological
canons, and it is through this lens that I came to explore the discipline
as a whole. Although I have never claimed to be a liberation theologian,
my research and teaching have been distinctly shaped by the theological
concerns placed in the foreground by authors from all over the globe
who are collectively identified as liberation theologians. These scholars
emphasize that the reflected faith experience of the oppressed, whether
that oppression is based on race, class, ethnocultural prejudice, sex, or
sexual identity, must be the starting point of theology.

It is therefore with great intellectual concern and personal sadness that
I have witnessed the increasing marginalization of liberation theology
in particular and theology as a whole. Commentaries about the failure,
irrelevance, and even death of liberation theologies abound. In a similar
vein, the role of theology within the university is increasingly contested.
This development is most often highlighted by the rigid and, I would
argue, false delineation between theology and religious studies.

The increasing irrelevance of theology to the academy as a whole and of liberation theologies to the theological academy is regrettable but not entirely surprising. Much of what is stated about liberation theologies today is true: they have failed to affect the dominant U.S. academy's understanding of the theological task; the poor are indeed poorer today than when the prophetic explosion of liberation theology occurred in the late 1960s and early 1970s; liberation theology has isolated itself from the broader U.S. religious studies academy. However, these challenges do not necessarily mean the demise of liberation theologies. Instead, they are invitations for them to grow. This book does not discuss the fact that liberation theologies written in the 1970s no longer have an impact on the contemporary church, world, and academy. Instead, it focuses on the present moment, arguing for the need to radically reconceptualize the theological task in order to answer the fundamental questions liberation theologians posed to us decades ago. Part of the recent problem for liberation theologies has been their reception in the United States. Other challenges include the construction of the Americas in isolation, instead of embracing a hemispheric approach to the Americas, as well as the rigid categories of identity that liberation theologians often espouse in their writings.[1] Yet another difficulty is the failure of many liberation theologians to write in a manner that reflects a connection to everyday Christians. Linked to this problem is the changing face of Christianity itself throughout the Americas, which is quite different from the Christianity often depicted in the pages of liberation theologies.

This book offers a critical introduction to scholarship on religion in the Americas by assessing the study of marginalized communities and the success of liberation theologies in context. To truly understand religion today, one needs to look to marginalized communities, those with which liberation theologies tend to be concerned, not just mainstream populations. Although eulogies for liberation theology have been published since the 1990s, theologians continue to write with a liberationist hermeneutic; meanwhile, on a parallel track, scholars in the United States from the fields of religious studies, anthropology, history, and sociology have begun to create an extensive corpus on the very populations that are the focus of liberation theologians. By drawing on a combination of historical and ethnographic sources, this book offers a new approach for theology, one that reflects direct grounding in the communities it claims to represent. This book argues that in order to remain relevant and useful theology needs to take into account how religion is actually experienced and to change the way it approaches its subject matter to contend with religion on the ground.

Defining Liberation Theology

The current religious landscape of the Americas contests common assertions made by liberation theologians that the religion of the oppressed is somehow liberationist and inherently ecclesial and Christian. The growth of Pentecostal and charismatic Christianity throughout the Americas, with their more conservative and apolitical theology, challenges the depiction of a highly politicized and socially progressive Christianity often found within liberationist texts. In a similar vein, liberation theologies tend to ignore the complexity of the American religious landscape, marginalizing indigenous and African religious traditions throughout the hemisphere.[2] This book questions whether liberation theology remains a useful category for academic discourse in religious studies, particularly in light of the field's commitment to justice broadly conceived. Whether scholars of religion should be advocates for the marginalized or infuse justice into their academic discourse is a hotly debated subject among scholars.

To fully understand, research, and teach religion in the Americas in general and that of the marginalized in particular, it is necessary to employ an interdisciplinary approach. Yet a chasm has slowly developed between those scholars who study religion from a theological perspective and those who approach the study of religion with a more interdisciplinary methodology. A core argument of this book is that this chasm needs to be bridged. It questions whether liberation theology alone can be an effective tool to describe the faith and religious life of marginalized communities and if it can empower them in their daily and societal struggles. It challenges theologians to adopt a more interdisciplinary approach and to engage with a variety of scholars who are working in the field of religious studies.

The focus of this volume is on liberation theologies within the complex interdisciplinary field of religious studies in the United States. This framing of liberation theology against the wider backdrop of the study of religion sets this introductory text apart from other overviews in the field, which often contextualize liberation theologies either in light of each other or solely in light of the ecclesial and social movements that inform them. Instead, this text contextualizes these theologies within the academic study of religion, offering a more comprehensive overview of the academic landscape from which these theologies emerge. Following this introduction, the book turns to case studies of the three liberation theologies—black theology, Latino/a theology, and Latin American theology—critically introducing them through an interdisciplinary overview of their dominant themes. This book introduces and furthers the conversation between theology and religious studies on religion in the Americas with an emphasis on marginalized populations.

Perhaps no other liberation theology has been more thoroughly dismissed and eulogized than the subject of Chapter One, Latin American liberation theology. Latin American theologians have generally made the error of interpreting their communities' religious rituals exclusively as liberationist in light of their sociopolitical context, yet they rarely examine the actual theology of these rituals, which is often far more theologically conservative. Moreover, Latin American theologians who claim a liberationist legacy must come to terms with the explosion of Pentecostalism and Charismatic Catholicism in the region. These Christian movements shy away from political engagement and structural critique. The growth of these movements counters the progressive

Christianity often depicted by liberation theologians. In addition, Latin American liberation theologians often do not reflect connections with actual lived communities in their scholarship. Their approach is in stark contrast to that of the numerous anthropologists and historians who have produced a body of literature grounded in Latin American religious communities. These scholars offer an alternative picture of religion in Latin America.

Chapter Two examines black liberation theology. The study of African American religion in the Americas has been marked by intentionally distinctive and parallel academic tracks. The field was born in the late 1960s through the writings of black liberation theologians who drew primarily from the Protestant Black Church tradition in the United States and from slave religion. This groundbreaking work was later debated and contested by second- and third-wave black theologians, who challenged the emphasis and scope of their predecessors. This critique and expansion of black theological discourse was followed by a parallel study of African American religion that appropriated an intentionally nontheological methodology. The work being done by religious studies scholars resonates far more with the lived religious experiences of African Americans. Many scholars who work in the field of African American religion have actively distanced themselves from their theological counterparts. This separation implies a critique of the theological lens as too narrow for studying African American religion in the United States and calls for a more interdisciplinary and interreligious approach.

Chapter Three turns to the writings of Latino/a theologians. Within the study of Latino/a religion one finds a theological discourse that does not often claim a liberationist hermeneutic but that allies itself closely with other liberationists and remains heavily grounded in the theo-ecclesial milieu. On a different path are those scholars who approach Latino/a religion from a historical and anthropological perspective. They do not explicitly distance themselves from their theologian colleagues; in many ways these two groups simply operate as if the other does not exist. Yet

Latino/a theology is heavily entrenched in Euro-American theology and thus often has little concrete connection to Latino/a religious communities. Too often what makes Latino/a theology Latino/a is its authorship. This mode of legitimation contrasts starkly with that of Latino/a scholars of religion whose research focus, not birthright, grounds the *latinidad* of their scholarship.

Following this overview of liberation theologies, Chapter Four turns in a more constructive direction by focusing on African diaspora religion as a starting point for pursuing an inclusive understanding of religion in the Americas. Scholars of African diaspora religion adopt an interdisciplinary methodology that places religion within the cross-section of race, ethnicity, and identity. In addition, the study of African diaspora religion throughout the Americas challenges the rigid lines drawn among black, Latino/a, and Latin American identities within liberation theologies. It also undermines the assumption that the religion of the marginalized in the Americas is exclusively Christian. African diaspora religions are a uniting presence among the three communities these theologies focus on in their research.

The Conclusion focuses on the study of religion in the Americas broadly conceived. Informed by the dialogue partners explored throughout this text this collaborative methodology presents a hemispheric approach that is most appropriate for discussing lived religious movements. Although not dismissive of liberation theologies, this approach is critical of their past and offers some challenges to their future as well as suggestions for preventing their untimely demise. It is clear that the liberation theologies of tomorrow cannot look like and may not be named in the same way as the liberation theologies of today.

In the spirit of liberation theology's emphasis on context, I must say a word about myself. As a Cuban American my scholarship has been shaped by the manner in which I have witnessed, participated in, and experienced religion among Cuban and Cuban American communities. My emphasis on African diaspora religions is a clear example of this approach, for this book could have been easily written with a focus on indigenous religious traditions. My focus on African diaspora religions is also based on their presence within the communities these three liberation theologies discuss in their corpus. In a similar vein, my desire to reconnect theology to the broader field of religious studies emerges from my own location as a trained theologian teaching in a department of religious studies at a secular university.

## Theology versus Religious Studies

The tenuous relationship between theology and religious studies has consistently marked debates within the academy surrounding the contemporary study of religion. Traditionally, and I would argue incorrectly, theology has been caricatured as fideistic claims about God that emerge from within a religious tradition. Given their association with particular religious traditions, the objectivity of theologians has been consistently questioned. This challenge is further amplified by many theologians' connections to their churches. Theology is associated with ecclesial advocacy and in the contemporary context has often been reduced to an apologetics within an academy that has grown increasingly disinterested in theology's truth claims. Religious studies, however, is associated with the detached and, therefore, objective and more scientific study of religion. It is seen as the more "academic" approach to religion, with more affinity to and relevance within the broader secular academy.

Religious studies emerges as distinct from theology as an outsider versus insider discipline. Yet religious studies is a discipline with no discipline; it is interdisciplinary, and although its interdisciplinary nature is a source of great creativity for the field, it also makes religious studies appear to lack cohesion. In addition, this is a field, unlike most others, whose scholars' academic credibility is based on our ability to distance ourselves from that which we study. Religious studies emerged by distinguishing itself from the predominance of theology and the Protestant influences that accompany it in the U.S. academy.

Protestant denominations' participation in the establishment of universities throughout the United States and in the often moralizing and ministerial role played by theological departments in those universities created a Protestant legacy. Separation from this legacy and the subsequent need to find broader academic credibility within the university signaled the first moment of what would come to be known as religious studies. The incorporation of the study of religion into the humanities within the university in the 1940s was based on its rupture from its Protestant legacy and its commitment to a more scientific approach. Coupled with the estrangement from Protestantism is the separation of scholars who claim to be theologians from those who embrace different methodological approaches to religion.[3] Yet this Protestant legacy continues to haunt religious studies because of the field's inability to provide a legitimate argument for its role in the academy in light of the modern disdain for the authority of religious institutions and the role of the supernatural in human life. The interdisciplinary nature of religious studies leads to departments in which colleagues have little in common: a religious studies department can be full of scholars who approach diverse religious traditions using disparate approaches. Couple this diversity with an inferiority complex that has resulted from claims that the religious studies academy is unscientific and one finds a distinctive position grounded in a sense that the subject matter of religion is somehow less serious than other subjects of study.

The distancing of religious studies from theology has also had an impact on the public voice of theologians. Theology has the double burden in the United States of working within a country in which religion is often considered a private affair and in which academic suspicions surrounding the nature of theology abound. Scholars who claim to work in religious studies tend to avoid theologians because their research contextualizes the study of religion within an interdisciplinary framework that engages the social, political, and cultural context of religion. Conversely, theology is often reduced to ecclesial concerns or hot-topic moral issues. The marginalization of theology emerges in part from the stances of theologians themselves: "In the academy, theology has mostly pursued its task apart from public scrutiny and in the company of theologians who apparently don't mind being cut off from interdisciplinary questioning. Theologians often produce work for religious readers with little regard for its intelligibility for nonreligious audiences and sociopolitical relevance in public life."[4] Although theology in the United States exists in a milieu in which religion is privatized, theologians themselves contribute to their own isolation. Theologians often engage in incestuous debates that have little relevance, and make little sense, outside of a small circle of academics. Who are theologians writing to and for? They are no longer writing for churches. And yet their academic community is limited. Are they writing only for themselves as a small group?

The relationship between theology and religious studies remains a hotly contested issue. Although many have pleaded for the ultimate separation or unification of the two, academics remain ambivalent about their relationship. In her 1999 American Academy of Religion (AAR) presidential address Margaret Miles argued for the demise of the distinction between theology and religious studies. "It is time, I believe, finally to lay to rest the debate over fundamental differences between 'theological studies' and the 'study of religion.'"[5] Miles continued, "Theological studies, thought of as exploring a religious tradition from within, must also bring critical questions to the tradition studied. And the study of religion, often described as taking an 'objective' or disengaged perspective, cannot be studied or taught without understanding the power and beauty, in particular historical situations, of the tradition or the author we study. Nor can religious studies avoid theology—the committed worldviews, beliefs, and practices of believers—by focusing on religious phénoménologies."[6] One should not polarize theology as subjective and religious studies as objective. Such distinctions are naïve and false. Theologians should always be critical of the tradition that they are studying, even if they are within it; scholars of religion who approach their subject matter without confronting the committed worldviews of those they study weaken their work. The study of religion cannot fall into the extremes of being either descriptive or confessional.

The conversation did not end with Miles's address, for two years later, in her own AAR presidential address, Rebecca Chopp noted, "Nearly every presidential speech of the last twenty years, for instance, has addressed the trenchant boundary between theological studies and religious studies as a founding conflict. What I mean by 'founding fratricidal conflict' is the social organization of the study of religion, produced and reproduced by theology and religious studies and by the attempts to overcome this split."[7] The academy is founded on this inescapable conflict, which will continue to define who we are as scholars of religion unless we imagine a new interdisciplinary space of engaged partnership. Chopp presents interdisciplinary conversations as the bridge that will heal the historic divide between theological and religious studies.

This denigration of theology as advocacy discourse for churches is of special relevance for liberation theologies. These theologies have always presented themselves as embodying a new method for doing theology. They have done so in part through the subject matter of their work, often broadly understood as being focused on those from the underside of history. Yet liberation theologians also argue that they embrace a new approach to theology, an interdisciplinary one that engages the broader academy more than theologies of the past have. This methodology is based on emphases on concrete social action within liberation theologies and the study of oppressed peoples and the conditions (social, historical, cultural, and political) that lead to their suffering. Liberation theologies offer a step in the right direction, though not to the extent called for by Chopp.

This interdisciplinary broadening of the theological task would seemingly be welcomed by the religious studies academy, yet it is accompanied by theocentric claims that are fundamental to liberation theologies and alien to religious studies scholars. Core to liberation theologies is an understanding of the Christian God as not neutral; as summarized by North American feminist theologian Elizabeth A. Johnson, "When people are ground down, this violates the way God wants the world to be. In response, the living God makes a dramatic decision: to side with oppressed peoples in their struggle for life."[8] Ultimately, the methodological shifts embraced by liberation theologians are still theological, based on their interpretation of the sacred. Liberation theologians interpret the suffering Christ in solidarity with, and some would even say as embodying, all suffering peoples. The resurrection contains within it the hope of liberation through Jesus's salvific death and resurrection. Liberation theology's emphasis on the marginalized is rooted in the nature of the sacred. What could be interpreted as a methodological shift that could open up theology via liberation theology's interdisciplinary approach becomes lost in theological claims justifying that methodology, thus ending the conversation before it even begins.

Linked to this marginalization is the role of advocacy both in liberation theologies in particular and in theology and in some cases religious studies in general. Both Chopp and Miles, in their presidential addresses, as well as a plethora of other liberation theologians and scholars of religion, define the study of religion as engaged scholarship. For Miles, part of the connection between the study of religion and theology is social engagement.[9] Chopp echoes Miles, connecting the significance of engaged scholarship to broader civic engagement, connecting education to the formation of citizenship in the United States.[10] Although this understanding of the scholar as advocate is fundamental to liberation theologies, it has not gained widespread acceptance among scholars of religion as a whole, in part because of the notion of the theologian as an advocate for the church. In fact, for some the engagement of the scholar, whether to a particular segment of the population or church or in a broader civic manner, is a point of debate within the academy.

Ultimately the question posed by those who argue for an intellectual moral imperative is, Are scholars of religion required to do engaged scholarship? In an op-ed for the *New York Times* Stanley Fish advises academics to do their job, namely to remain ivory tower academics. Taking on the Marxist impulse that informs many liberation theologians, Fish argues, "Marx famously said that our job is not to interpret the world, but to change it. In the academy, however, it is exactly the reverse: our job is not to change the world, but to interpret it."[11] Fish contends that because the task of the academic is challenging enough, academics do their job best when they are focused on the academy. Social change should not be the goal of academic life.

An entirely contrasting approach is embraced by African American public intellectual Michael Eric Dyson, who argues for the fundamental commitment of the intellectual. An academic is different from an intellectual. For Dyson, an academic is someone who does his or her job, but to be an intellectual is a vocation. An intellectual is someone who is broad based and interdisciplinary in his or her scholarship, refusing to be "disciplined" by the categories of academic subjects.[12] Dyson argues that the intellectual plays a role in relieving suffering and has an obligation to be committed to the common good. Some may argue that Dyson's description of the intellectual—a description that many liberation theologians, scholars of religion, and Chopp and Miles would embrace—downplays the scientific objectivity of the academy. Yet Dyson reminds us that knowledge is not neutral. The connection of power and knowledge is of great concern for Dyson: it sets the stage for the role of advocacy for intellectuals, a claim Fish would contest. Liberation theologians also argue passionately for engaged scholarship, yet they seem to do so unaware of these broader debates within the academy. They do not recognize how engaged scholarship may weaken the academic credibility of their work in some circles.

Presidential addresses such as those of Miles and Chopp have led some to claim that organizations such as the AAR are not welcoming places for the scientific study of religion because of their rejection of objective or neutral scholarship. They have historically defined the task of religious studies as engaged scholarship, marginalizing any sort of disinterested approach as ideological in its own right.[13] According to these critics, religious studies scholars are not as objective as they claim to be, for they have overwhelmingly accepted the subjectivity of their scholarship, and this subjectivity threatens the academic credibility of the field of religion. "A study of religion directed toward spiritual liberation of the individual or of the human race as a whole, toward the moral welfare of the human race, or toward an ulterior end than that of knowledge itself, should not find a role in the university; for if allowed in, its sectarian concerns will only contaminate the quest for a scientific knowledge of religions and eventually undermine the very institution from which it originally sought legitimation."[14] While I disagree with this sentiment, it is important to recognize this critique of engaged scholarship. Of concern is not only the methodology of religious studies but, when theology is thrown into the mix, the question of authority. Who defines the agenda of theology: the academy or the church?

The question of authority is a fundamental one for the future of liberation theology in the Americas. The three theologies explored in this book have made distinctive claims about the authoritative voices in their scholarship and the nature of religious authority within their communities. Latin American liberation theology has drawn primarily from the voices of marginalized Christian communities and an understanding of the Christian church as the church of the poor. This claim has led to clashes with the institutional hierarchy of the Roman Catholic Church. Black liberation theology roots its claims in the Black Church, a broadly constructed and, some would argue, false category that represents black Christianity as a whole in the United States. Latino/a theologians tend to take the popular Christian practices of Christian Latino/a faith communities as their starting point. They define these practices as popular based on their relationship with institutional Catholicism. In all these theologies there is a dynamic between institutional religious authority and the religious authority of everyday Christians. The question becomes, therefore, whether this dynamic somehow weakens the academic nature of these theological voices.

Although claims surrounding the weakened academic credibility of theology because of ecclesial authority are somewhat simplistic in their understanding of theology, there is something distinctive about the study of religion in relationship to other academic disciplines. Religious studies is marked by the polarities of praxis and critical reflection.[15] Within this space of imagination is the engaged scholar, who may in the study of religion have a moral imperative to justice that shapes his or her scholarship. The polarity of religious practice can become the rub, for it can be construed as weakening critical analysis. Can a believer be truly critical of his or her religion in the same manner as an outsider? Can an outsider truly understand a religious worldview she or he does not believe? These are not easy questions, and they go to the root of the struggles liberation theologies confront today. They are also at the root of debates within the field of religion. Theologians are not the only ones who want to maintain their academic credibility and simultaneously acknowledge the subjective dimension of their scholarship.

## Lived Religion

Within the study of U.S. religion scholars who are loosely grouped by their emphasis on lived religion are interesting conversation partners for liberation theologians. Scholars who embrace the lived-religion approach use social history as a methodology for American religious history. "The name for this approach is 'lived religion,' a shorthand phrase that has long been current in the French tradition of the sociology of religion (*la religion veçue*) but is relatively novel in the American context. . . . The phrase is rooted less in sociology than in cultural and ethnographic approaches to the study of religion and American religious history that have come to the fore in recent years."[16] Central to this methodology is the notion that the study of American religion can be enhanced through interdisciplinary studies. These scholars distance themselves from the term *popular religion*, often used to describe the religion of the "people," a category used by Latin American and

Latino/a liberation theologians. The "people" of popular religion usually refers to the poor and marginalized. The manner in which popular religion plays a role in liberation from marginalization is a contested topic among Latino/a and Latin American theologians. The emphasis on lived versus popular religion is grounded in part on the assumption that the category of popular religion creates an oppositional relationship between official and popular religious practices. The lived-religion approach embraces the significance of daily life situated within broader institutional and social networks. Fundamental to the understanding of lived religion is the individual nature of everyday religious practices that occur within an intersubjective social framework.[17] The lived-religion approach attempts to balance contextualized religious practices in light of institutional and historical movements.

Sociohistorian Robert Orsi, a leading voice in the study of lived religion, presents this methodology as having broad implications for the study of religion as a whole. Orsi advocates for the reconfiguration of the study of religion through an awareness of the possibilities and limitations of culture; an awareness of the role of the body in particular cultures; and an awareness of the structures of social experience and the tensions that can disrupt these structures. He defines the approach as a "materialist phenomenology of religion," where "scholars of 'lived religion' seek a more dynamic integration of religion and experience."[18] This approach allows for the improvisational nature of religion to thrive. It argues that the opposition of elite and popular is an oversimplification, for religion is experienced within the exchange between religious authorities and communities of faith.[19] This emphasis on everyday, material religion is sympathetic to many of the concerns highlighted by liberation theologians.

Scholars of lived religion are already engaged in dialogue with liberation theologies. For example, Sarah McFarland Taylor, author of *Green Sisters: A Spiritual Ecology*, embraces a lived-religion methodology informed by a feminist hermeneutic. She embraces the feminist call for a "view from below," at the grassroots level, versus the perspective of the hierarchical, institutional elite. McFarland Taylor strives for a reciprocal, horizontal relationship, with the researcher acquiring "spectator knowledge" through active participation as part of the research process.[20] The objects of study cease to be others. Her approach is dominated by the desire to study "religion on the ground," which examines how individuals in their daily lives practice their beliefs. McFarland Taylor emphasizes that this methodology is particularly significant for the study of women in religion.[21] Her book is an ethnographic study of green sisters (environmentally active catholic nuns) supplemented by written materials using "interlocking sources" in order to uncover when "patterns emerged across multiple sources."[22] McFarland Taylor's scholarship brings together a number of significant intersections that liberation theologians also address: institutional and everyday religious practices, the function of power, and, perhaps most important, the role of the academic in the study of religion.

The lived-religion approach, however, is not without its own methodological constraints, particularly in regard to voice: "The confessional mode, too, introduces epistemological and moral problems. It claims authority just as it pretends to undercut it. It does so by implying that the author has privileged information about his or her own motives and location, persuading the reader that the writer has come clean." This mode does not necessarily lead to the erasure of the autobiographical voice, yet it has its limitations.[23] Liberation theologians' strident emphasis on the significance of context, culture, and social location often reduces their contributions to parochial voices lost in the larger framework of religious and theological discourse. This book resists the either-or dualisms surrounding religious practices and discourses that plague the contemporary academy. A hybrid language must not reify the dualism of religious studies and theology, of insider and outsider, but must recognize instead that the divide between the two is a false construction.

Some connections already exist, such as the emphasis on material, everyday religion that is found in the work of some contemporary social historians and liberation theologians. Fundamental for these scholars are the significance of everyday religion and the contributions of everyday individuals to academic discourse. The privileging of nonexperts is not a dismissal of academic discourse and institutional authority. However, the study of everyday religion creates a space for the privileged and nonprivileged, the private and the public.[24] This emphasis on the nonprivileged and nonexpert echoes the centrality of grassroots, everyday individuals at the heart of liberation theologies. It appears that some scholars of lived religion have a starting point similar to that of liberation theologians, although they have an entirely different approach and academic commitment.

Is lived religion therefore the middle ground between theology and religious studies? Ultimately no. The lived-religion approach is not the exclusive remedy for the ambiguous relationship between theology and religious studies. The lived-religion approach often leaves scholars wanting more. Although it acknowledges the significance of social historians' descriptions of religious experiences and devotions, the desire to pose critical questions and impose critical analyses on these devotions remains a strong impulse in the academic study of religion. Lived religion, though broadening the field of religious studies, still remains embedded within it, hesitant to reflect on the theology implied by the religious practices scholars study. Collaborations with theologians could fill this void. Although many of the critiques of liberation theologies, for example the lack of concrete connection to everyday religious practices, could be answered by adopting a more empirical and materialist approach, doing so must never be at the expense of the significance of theology. It is not that liberation theologians should stop being theologians; rather, they need to radically reconceive the theological task and broaden their academic audience. A collaborative approach would strengthen and challenge both methodologies.

A dialogue between scholars of lived religion and theologians would be a fruitful space in which to explore some of the broader debates surrounding subjectivity and engagement within the field of religion.

Does an ethnographic study of a marginalized community that sets out the concerns and struggles of this community qualify as engaged scholarship? Is it the same type of engaged scholarship as a theologian's claim that God is on the side of the oppressed? Does the mere act of highlighting oppression make a scholar engaged? Similarly, the issue of authorship within the study of religion is a pressing question that continues to haunt the field. Scholars of lived religion force us to (rightfully) entertain the notion that all academic research is ultimately autobiographical. There can be no objective study of religion or study of any subject for that matter. The author as interpreter is always present in the text.

For liberation theologians the question of authorship is repeatedly raised. Given that liberation theologies have consistently claimed that they represent the theological insights of marginalized peoples, assessment of their efficacy and their impact is complex. One cannot reduce the presence of theologians to the presence of the people they claim to represent. The presence of liberationist voices within the academy should not be the criteria for determining whether marginalized peoples have intellectual insights for the study of religion, and the sales of books by liberation theologians should not determine whether we can define contemporary religion in the Americas without taking seriously the majority of peoples in this hemisphere. And yet too often the whims of the academy define the agenda.

## Liberation Theology: Does Marginalization = Death?

The marginalization and sometimes discrediting of liberation theologies is often equated with their death. Yet academic eulogies for liberation theology, particularly Latin American liberation theology, are often based on contemporary political and economic factors rather than theological standing. The collapse of socialism symbolized by the breakup of the Soviet Union and the emergence of the United States as a global

hegemonic capitalist superpower has contributed greatly to the perceived demise of liberation theology, particularly in Latin America. Yet
this perceived failure does not warrant the smothering of liberationist
concerns.[25]

One of the elements that contributes to the marginalization of liberation theologies is their reduction to contextual or advocacy theologies.
Cast as contextual theologies, they become special-interest theologies that
are relevant only to specific groups. Yet Euro-American liberation theologian Jeorg Rieger reminds us that, given their emphasis on oppression,
liberation theologies are distinct from contextual theologies. "There is
still too little awareness that context may not be what is closest to home,
but that what needs attending is 'what hurts' and what lies below the
surface. One of the great advantages of the various liberation theologies
over contextual theology is that they are trying to deal with context as that
which hurts."[26] Often understood as advocacy theologies, they are seen as
catering exclusively to the interests of specific groups.[27] Liberation theologies are perceived as ministering mainly to the interest of specific groups
of different ethnic, gender, or class origins, allowing what is considered
authentic or normative theology to continue untouched by the challenges
raised by liberation theologians. Liberation theologies become projects on
the margins, read only when the needs of a particular group are the focus.
They are not seen as affecting dominant theology as a whole.

In addition to external critiques of liberation theologies, significant
internal analyses have been pushing liberation theologians to critically
engage their own discourse for decades. The late Latin American liberation theologian Marcela Althaus-Reid is critical of the notion of the
popular theologian, the academic who has a close relationship with and
often translates the world of the poor to the academy. Within liberation theology the popular theologian is constructed as a "mirror" of the
poor, a reflection of the faith of the poor. Academic theologians become
the voice of the voiceless, infantilizing the very communities they are
attempting to empower through their theological commitments. The

popular theologian becomes a hybrid academic/representative of the poor who filters the horrors of marginalization in a sanitized manner to the U.S. academy.[28] The caricature of the popular theologian becomes a conceptual construct that results in the co-optation and consequent powerlessness of liberation theologies in the face of dominant Western discourse. Popular theologians are usually priests or ministers living with and working with the poor whose faith, suffering, and simplicity are acclaimed.[29] Such theologians become infantilized for their humility and dedication to the poor while their intellectual claims to the discourse of theology remain unheard. Their value to the dominant academy is not intellectual; it is voyeuristic.

Althaus-Reid's critique of the popular theologian is coupled with her insight into the manner in which liberation theologies become "theme parks" that Western theologians can visit while not having to alter the nature and structure of their theology. As theme-park theologies, she contends, liberation theologies become a commodity for Western capitalism. "The centerpiece of theological thinking is constituted by systematic Western theology, and it is done even in opposition. The theme parks, in the case of Liberation Theology, are divided into subthemes, such as 'Marxist Theology', 'Evangelical Theology', 'Indigenous Theology', or 'Feminist Theology'—and all of them with a central unifying theme ending with 'and the poor.'"[30] As theme parks, they can be visited at one's leisure; one is never forced to take them seriously. They do not affect the center, the dominant discourse of theology. A huge challenge to liberation theologies as a whole in the United States is that liberals claim that they accept liberation theology without embracing the liberationist method. Liberation theology has failed to transform the nature and method of theology as a whole.

Another internal critique within liberation theology argues that it has lost its vitality in the contemporary academy. The next generation of liberation theologians is challenged. "The question for the next generation is whether we should move beyond the discourse of liberation or refine rhetoric, goals, and methods of the movement to reflect current issues."[31] Ultimately underlying this critique is the question of whether one can "do" liberation theology but call it something different. Liberation theologians often homogenize the lived experiences of oppressed peoples with broad sweeping claims about them. They also claim that a shared experience of oppression is enough to unite marginalized peoples.[32] All minorities are classified as those seeking liberation; differences among them are effaced. By highlighting the experience of oppressed communities, liberation theologians have reduced these communities to the experience of oppression. This diminution has created an ahistorical notion of oppression entirely disconnected from concrete communities. This idea not only has severed the relationship between the theologian and lived religious communities but also has erased the distinctiveness and diversity of the manner in which oppression manifests itself.

In order to respond to their critics, and more important, to be true to their intellectual commitments, liberation theologians need to reconnect with lived religious communities. The future of liberation theology lies in this relationship. Disconnected from concrete communities, its center has moved to the academy.[33] If liberation theologians choose to embrace an understanding of theology that is merely academic, then they break radically with their foremothers and forefathers. Today one finds a lack of deep connection between the writings of most liberation theologians and concrete faith communities. If that connection is there, it is not apparent from reading these authors' works.

Liberation theologies must deal with the question of accountability and theological ownership. How ought liberation theologians write about religious communities and expressions with which they do not agree or that they do not like or find liberatory? Whose experience will be the subject of theology? "Experience" here does not mean personal experience, but taking the concreteness of everyday life seriously. Is one of the issues liberation theologies' failure to connect their theological commitments to the ecclesial traditions from which they emerge? Liberation theologians have also not sufficiently addressed the assumed normativity of Christianity in their writings. Many aspects of concrete, lived Christianity become abstractly accepted within broader theological currents.[34]

The questions posed throughout this text are ones that need to be asked of theology as a discipline and of the study of religion as a whole. We are living in a moment when the significance of religion in shaping world events is more prominent than ever, and yet the study of religion remains a marginalized and inconsequential field. Scholars of religion must become advocates for their discipline or it will fade away into irrelevance. However, the multidimensional nature of religion makes this project extremely complex. For the theologian, the question of authority and voice becomes central. Theologians have a significant contribution to make, yet they often become lost in internal debates on the nature of theology. Theologians need to find a way to communicate to nontheologians. At the same time, religious studies scholars should shake off their inferiority complex regarding their place in the humanities and develop a stronger sense of their role in the academy, a vision that must include theology as one avenue for studying religion. Liberation theologians in particular must be honest about the nature of their claims and recognize that their "revolutionary" incorporation of the social sciences has been in fact a very narrow appropriation of certain perspectives within the social sciences.

Ultimately the starting point of liberation theology is not ethics or social theory; it is a theological vision of the sacred embodied in concrete faith communities. Liberation theology must remain deeply connected to social movements for it to survive. At its core, liberation theology can never be exclusively academic. A final question I will pursue throughout this text, one that goes to the heart of the challenge of liberation theologians, is, Is the challenge of liberation theology methodological or theocentric? Or is it epistemological? In other words, what are the roots of the radical transformation liberation theologians propose for the discipline of theology as whole? The answer to these questions will have implications not only for the future of liberation theologies but also for their ability to dissolve the divide between theology and religious studies, as well as that between the Americas.

# 1

## Latin American Liberation Theology

Latin American liberation theology, born in the late 1960s, argues that nonpersons, the poor and oppressed, must be the starting point and center of theological reflection. A theology that does not begin with the faith, life, and struggles of those from the underside of history is not a true Christian theology.[1] Latin American liberation theology functions on three levels: the popular, the pastoral, and the academic.[2] The first two give life to academic reflection: the spirituality and political praxis of grassroots Christian communities informs theoretical theological reflection. Grounded in the belief that economic and social justice are the center of Christianity's mission, this Latin American theological movement has created a radical new ecclesial reality that centers on grassroots Christian communities and an innovative vision of the theological task. The Roman Catholic emphasis on the preferential option for the poor speaks to the global, institutional impact of this movement. However, in spite of the many publications, the pastoral life, and the pedagogy that center on this theology, rumblings have grown in the halls of the academy regarding the "death" and "failure" of liberation theology, even to the point of discussing postliberation theologies.

Academic liberation theology, admittedly, has become increasingly detached from the everyday lives of ecclesial Christians. In addition, the explosion of Pentecostalism in Central and South America and the

Caribbean offers an alternative ecclesial model contrary to the Church of the poor celebrated by liberation theologians, which emphasizes political and social engagement. Nonetheless, the notion that the era of liberation theology is past and its effectiveness undermined is untrue. Such critiques emerge from a detached academy that is disconnected from the lives of grassroots communities within the Latin American Church. Proclamations of the death of liberation theologies in general are unfortunate as they lead to a disregard for oppressed peoples and to their increasing marginalization in the contemporary context. Just because for some observers Latin American liberation theology has "failed" to transform the nature of the theological task—although it has in fact radically transformed theological discourse—does not mean that we can forget the concrete lives and struggles of those who are at the center of this theological movement.

## Ecclesial and Academic Roots

Before discussing the intellectual and social movements that fed the birth of Latin American liberation theology, it is important to contextualize it within the ecclesial milieu of Latin America. Our focus here is the contemporary era, Christianity in the twentieth and twenty-first centuries, with an emphasis on Christian movements that heavily involve the laity within Catholic circles and on the growth of Protestantism throughout the continent. Three elements that characterize Latin American Christianity frame the discussion: Catholic lay movements, base Christian communities, and the growth of *movimientos evangélicos* both in Roman Catholic and in Protestant circles.[3] These movements reflect a grassroots approach to Latin American Christianity that emphasizes the everyday religion of Latin American Christians. Moreover, these three elements form bridge movements between institutional and what is often described as popular Catholicism. Popular Catholicism refers to the religious practices of the masses that are often, but not always, in tension with the institutional Roman Catholic Church. Local devotions to the saints and Mary, religious processions, and domestic religion are examples of popular Catholicism. Popular Catholicism is a subset within the category of popular religion.

Twenty-first century Christianity in Latin America inherited a legacy of colonial Catholicism that was linked to the oppressive regime of the Spanish empire and its conquest of the Americas. As a result of this history, once Latin American countries gained independence from Spain, the Church was faced with liberal governments that promoted staunch anticlericalism, and it was forced to align itself with conservative factions in the nineteenth and early twentieth centuries. Also of note is the historical lack of indigenous clergy within Latin American countries, where priests and women religious were predominantly foreign born. In addition, a shortage of priests throughout Latin America led to a population that was well schooled in popular Catholicism and religiosity yet was not thoroughly instructed in dogmatic theological teachings. A distinctive Latin American Catholicism emerged, composed of a mixture of indigenous and African religions with Catholic elements; the growth of this kind of Catholicism was due, in part, to the lack of a strong clerical presence. The nature of the Catholic Church's presence as a dominant religious and political force, coupled with the absence of the ecclesial Church in the daily lives of many Latin Americans, also left fertile ground for the growth of Protestantism and the survival of indigenous and African religions.

Roman Catholic lay movements were born in Latin America in the early twentieth century. Their purpose was threefold: defense of Catholicism in the face of anti-Catholic governments, encouragement of Catholic culture, and promotion of social justice. Movements such as Catholic Action emerged from an apologetic Catholicism with an eye toward promoting Catholic social teachings. Catholic Action sought to promote lay leadership in the Church globally and was very active in Latin America. The intention was for lay people to influence the secular realm with Catholic values. Catholic Action utilized a "see-judge-act" methodology that encouraged adherents to describe the world around them, to assess that world in light of Catholic principles, and to respond with concrete action. Catholic Action was an essential dimension of twentieth-century Latin American Catholicism.

Another significant lay movement was the Cursillos de Cristiandad. The Cursillos began as exclusively male gatherings in order to encourage lay men to become more active in the Church. However, after much petitioning women were allowed to participate. Cursillos are gatherings of thirty to forty lay people, directed by a layperson and with a priest serving as spiritual advisor. They usually take the form of a three-day retreat that combines music, silence, and reflection. Underlying the *cursillo* movement was a desire to train a new lay leadership within local churches.

Base Christian Communities (BCCs) were yet another means of promoting such leadership. Perhaps no other dimension of the Latin American Church in the twentieth century is more well-known than these communities. The birth of BCCs may be traced to 1963, when North American priest Leo Mahon led a group of priests from Chicago to Panama City to run an adult ministry program. This became a focal point for BCCs, and hundreds of clergy, women religious, and laity came to explore and model this community effort. The "base" of Base Christian Communities refers to both the socioeconomic and internal structure of BCCs.[4] BCCs are also referred to as CEBs (*comunidades eclesiales de base*). They are small religious groups typically consisting of friends and neighbors; most often they were initiated by members of the institutional Church (priests, lay leaders). BCCs combine religiosity, such as bible study and prayer, with community activism. Although many understand these communities as geared entirely toward leftist political activism, their theological and political bent varies significantly.[5] They also vary dramatically in parish structure and the priest with which they coexist.

The key point is that BCCs are not distinct from the institutional Church but instead are a natural development within it that centers on lay participation and leadership.[6] Part of the appeal and success of BCCs is that, because of their small size, these communities have a strong spirit of communitarianism and lack institutionalization. Institutionalization, in fact, would lead to the death of the communitarian spirit. "Church" is not limited to the institutionalized mass but occurs when a community gathers in discipleship to celebrate Jesus Christ. BCCs constitute the Church despite the absence of clergy and the Eucharistic within them. As theologian Leonardo Boff emphasizes, the historical weakness of the institutional church contributed in part to the establishment of BCCs. "It is not that this absence is not felt, is not painful. It is, rather, that these ministers do not exist in sufficient numbers. The historical situation does not cause the church to disappear. The church abides in the people of God as they continue to come together, convoked by the word and discipleship of Jesus Christ."[7] BCCs, however, are not in conflict or competition with the institutional church. The communitarian aspect of BCCs is instead a source of institutional renewal. The two, communitarian and institutional, must coexist together. Ultimately, liberation theologians argue, BCCs represent the true Church of the poor. "Thus, we are no longer speaking of the Church *for* the poor but rather a Church *of* and *with* the poor."[8] The grassroots nature of BCCs as the church of the masses reveals them as being constituted by and in solidarity with poor Latin Americans.

The contributions of BCCs are significant, albeit at times saturated with a romanticism and idealization that perhaps led to the downfall of the idea of BCCs in academic circles This idealization is seen both in the description of the base communities themselves and in the exaggeration of their numbers. Also, not all scholarship on BCCs paints the extensive and favorable picture given by most liberation theologians. Although early liberation theologians depicted BCCs in a utopian manner, social scientists have painted a different picture, recognizing that many BCCs had their origins in the institutional church and were sanctioned and encouraged by ecclesial leaders.[9] In other words, BCCs were much more intimately linked to the institutional church than many liberation theologians implied. The widespread nature of BCCs has been contested, with some studies stating that both liberation theology and BCCs affected less than 5 percent of the Catholic population in Latin America. Their presence, success, and/or failure must be studied at the regional level, for their influence varies significantly depending on country and region.[10] One movement, however, that is gaining widespread support throughout Latin America—and among Latino/as in the United States—is the *evangélico* movement.

Perhaps no other religious movement within Latin America has received more recent attention by academics than the growth of Pentecostal churches. Pentecostalism should be framed in light of the broader spread of evangelical Christianity throughout the region. Recent figures estimate that at least one in ten Latin Americans are evangelical, with 70–80 percent Pentecostal. In some countries the figures are even higher. The indigenous nature of Pentecostalism, with its Latin American pastors and leadership, is its greatest resource. In other words, unlike Catholicism, in which the clergy is often foreign born, Pentecostalism and other Protestant *evangélico* movements draw their leadership from the local population. Pentecostalism, neo-Pentecostalism, and Charismatic Catholicism, a movement within the Roman Catholic Church that shares many similarities with Pentecostalism, exploded globally in the second half of the twentieth century. The term *evangélico* is used in Latin America to loosely categorize all Protestants, although it is often used by scholars to describe the more theologically and socially conservative branches of Protestantism. Pentecostalism in Latin America often has a twofold structure: churches that have emerged with denominational ties to North American churches or indigenous churches that exist as independent entities.

Characteristics of *evangélico* belief include the authority of Scripture, the experience of personal salvation through Jesus Christ, and the importance of the missionary enterprise.[11] It is too simplistic to assume that the growth of evangelicalism in Latin America is due to North American evangelization efforts and money. This assumption also downplays the religious ownership of evangelicalism by the poor. Most important, as previously suggested, the opportunities for native pastoral leadership became one of evangelical Protestantism's greatest appeals. Unlike Catholic clergy, evangelical pastors are not required to pursue higher education, and thus ecclesial leadership much more accessible to the poor in Protestant denominations. Also, there are more possibilities at the local level because of the variety and number of evangelical churches. If one has a dispute with a pastor, one can go to or even start a new church.

Pentecostalism has emerged as an unlikely source of empowerment for women. This development is due in part to the manner in which Pentecostalism reconfigures the line between public and private life; it encourages men to become more active in the domestic sphere than they usually are. In contrast, liberationist Catholicism has tended to emphasize the public and the structural at the expense of oppressive paradigms within the domestic sphere.[12] Evangelical movements within Christianity build on the importance of the personal and the domestic for religious life. One of Pentecostalism's greatest appeals has been the manner in which it directly addresses the everyday struggles of families and communities especially in regard to social issues such as alcoholism and gambling.

Often when one thinks of *movimientos evangélicos* in Latin America, the assumption is that these movements are exclusively Protestant. However, the Catholic Charismatic Renewal movement (CCR) is the evangelical face of Catholicism. The CCR is the fastest growing movement in Latin American Catholicism; and Latin America is the region with the greatest increase in the CCR globally.[13] The CCR was born in 1966 at Duquesne University in Pittsburgh. The movement spread to Latin America in the 1970s. CCR's first members were predominantly middle class and included a large number of women. Three trends shaped the movement during the 1980s: growth among the popular classes, episcopal approval, and its primacy as a tool of evangelization. In the 1990s CCR became institutionalized. CCR not only is one of the largest and fastest growing movements in the Latin American Church but also is thriving in other parts of the global South. It has enormous appeal among the laity and has the approval of national episcopacies. Nevertheless, the movement has received scant academic attention, in part because of scholars' heavy emphasis on liberation theology and BCCs. One of the factors that distinguishes the CCR is its missionary appeal and its use of media. Although ecclesial leaders were at first hesitant about accepting this strong lay movement, its heavy emphasis on ecclesial submission quickly earned the episcopacy's approval.

Another feature that marks Charismatic Catholicism is its similarity to Pentecostalism, as seen in the shared emphasis on the Holy Spirit. "That both U.S. and Latin American Charismatics initially called themselves Pentecostal Catholics is revealing. Catholic Charismatics share the same ecstatic spirituality with Protestant Pentecostals. Like Pentecostals, Catholic Charismatics are pneumocentrists; that is, the Holy Spirit occupies center stage in believers' religious practice."[14] This emphasis on the Holy Spirit distinguishes Charismatics from other Catholic groups. A belief in the gifts of the Spirit, such as faith healing and glossolalia; a certain degree of biblical fundamentalism; and asceticism are some of the characteristics Charismatics share with Pentecostals. Devotion to Mary and acquiescence to the Vatican, however, are distinguishing markers of the CCR in contrast to Pentecostalism. While seeing the CCR as a way of combating Protestantism, many clergy were concerned that its pneumocentrism would undermine ecclesial authority. The CCR is characterized by weekly prayer groups (*grupos de oración*) that can include as few as ten or as many as three hundred members. Lay leaders direct them, and priests do not often participate. A diversity of prayer forms can be found within Charismatic Catholicism, including hymns, glossolalia, and pneumatic praise.[15] Unlike the clergy-led mass, therefore, lay Charismatic Catholics are empowered to find authority within themselves. They combine mass media with a pneumocentric, biblically oriented Catholicism that maintains the significance of Mary and consequently its connection to the institutional Church.[16] The clerical hierarchy does not perceive the CCR as challenging institutional structures or excessively emphasizing political engagement.

The growth of evangelical Protestant movements in Latin America is often highlighted as an indicator of Catholicism's increasing demise within these countries. Various factors have contributed to the growth of these movements in general. Although the Catholic Church's failure to root itself in the region has certainly added to its diminution, blaming this development on the growth of Protestant movements is inadequate. One should also take into consideration the internal dynamics of church communities, the change in the religious environment, and the current sociopolitical context. In addition to these factors, a move to a more spiritualized pastoral work is a key factor.[17] Many of the problems the Catholic Church in Latin America faces today are institutional: "Latin American parishes are weak in organization and in many places, have little impact on the lives of those who live in their neighborhoods. . . . True, many Latin Americans are emotionally tied to the Church. But in participation, knowledge, and ethics, Catholicism is the religion of a minority.[18] This larger history, both social and intellectual, is fundamental for understanding Catholicism in Latin America in general and liberation theology in particular.

The growth of evangelical Christianity within Latin America challenges liberation theologians to recast how they understand the faith of the poor. One characteristic of Pentecostalism and Charismatic Catholicism is a stronger emphasis on everyday life and spirituality than on broader social issues.[19] In Pentecostalism this deemphasis on the political is based in part on its soteriology, which anticipates the impending return of Christ and thus precludes long-term political engagement.[20] In many ways, this situation creates some core questions for liberation theologians: How will liberation theologians' theologies be transformed if they write about Christians who do not see an automatic connection between their faith and broader social structures? Will liberation theologians ignore those Christians and write only about Christian communities that embody the academic principles of theologians? What kind of Christianity is truly liberative? Who answers these questions, the academics or the people?

For Catholic Latin American liberation theologians, the growth of Charismatic Catholicism is an important ecclesial reality. The CCR has been extremely successful in Latin America, in part because of the Vatican's view that it is a means of revitalizing the church. Unlike progressive Catholics, who understand social change as a natural expression of their faith, many Charismatics believe that evangelization is central. Another distinction is that although progressive Catholics want to democratize and share leadership in the local parishes, Charismatic Catholicism emphasizes ecclesial and hierarchical authority.[21] The CCR challenges constructions of Latin American Catholicism and the manner in which liberation theologians depict the political and social commitments of the poor.

Progressive Catholicism as a whole is at a crossroads in Latin America. Although adherents have managed to spread their programs and concerns throughout Latin America, they have failed to become strongly institutionalized. New social movements are rising that deal with more contextual, local issues: "These movements press the state for a decentralization of power and also challenge traditional opposition actors such as trade unions, leftist political parties and the Catholic Church. . . . Many new social movements retain strong religious bases, but their affiliations are likely to be diverse, encompassing not only Catholicism but also Pentecostal Protestantism and African-based religions, among others."[22] This move toward more localized social movements that are interreligious is increasingly the new face of religious activism in the region, one which liberation theology should draw from as a resource. The study of these movements will challenge many of the assumptions held by liberation theologians regarding Christian praxis and ecclesial life.

Sociologist Christian Smith, in *The Emergence of Liberation Theology: Radical Religion and Social Movement Theory*, provides a substantial sociological overview of the broader global and intellectual currents that led to the birth and growth of Latin American liberation theology.[23] His study is significant for its contextualization of Latin American liberation theology in light of global Christianity. Smith rightfully argues that one cannot understand the development of liberation theology in Latin America without understanding the broader ecclesial, popular, and intellectual strands that inform this theology. In the 1930s, the Latin American Church began the "New Christendom" project, which sought to establish the Catholic Church as a major institutional and cultural influence on the creation of a modern Latin America. However, because of the growing critique of capitalism, this project failed by the 1960s. The early 1950s also marked important moments for the development of Latin American liberation theology. In 1952, the CNBB (National Conference of Brazilian Bishops) was founded. The Latin American Episcopal Council (CELAM) was founded in 1955, the same year its first meeting in Rio de Janeiro occurred.

Smith highlights the importance of Catholic social teachings for the development of Latin American liberation theology. Through this and other intellectual currents Smith reveals the European influences on Latin American theological and social movements. Nouvelle Théologie in Europe, for example, sought to put the Church in contact with the modern world and was a precursor to Vatican II. Pope Paul VI's *Populum Progressio*, issued in 1967, takes an extremely strong stand on social issues. The see-judge-act method, often attributed exclusively to Latin American thinkers, was in fact designed in the 1940s by Catholic Action. This method is fundamental for understanding the theology of foundational figure Gustavo Gutiérrez, who is considered by many the "father" of Latin American liberation theology. Gutiérrez's book *A Theology of Liberation* embraced this approach, and it is considered the first monograph within Latin American liberation theology.[24]

Catholic Action was a significant precursor of liberation theology. Gutiérrez was a member of Catholic Action groups, and this involvement was one of the factors that led to his international acclaim.[25] Catholic Action created a space for lay mobilization in Peru and made connections between religion and politics. Catholic Action also created a set of networks that would be vital for liberationist movements in the 1960s and 1970s. In 1971 Gutiérrez and others founded the Bartolomé de las Casas

Institute, which provided summer courses for pastoral leaders, social activists, and intellectuals. Between 1971 and 1987 attendance jumped from two hundred to twenty-five hundred. These workshops contributed directly to Gutiérrez's writings, as witnessed in *We Drink from Our Own Wells*.[26]

Although Latin American liberation theology claims to represent a revolutionary break from European modes of theological thinking, many of the first Latin American liberation theologians were educated in Europe and were influenced by European-born Catholic social movements. Although it is related to European theology, Latin American liberation theology is distinct: "It is the theology of a colonial or neocolonial world which often simply reflects the theology of the 'center'; but in its more creative moments it has produced a new theology that has risen up against the great traditionally constituted theology."[27] Latin American theology has an ambiguous relationship with the European center that aided in its birth and growth. This tension between the European legacy and the commitment to the everyday faith of the Latin American poor continues to haunt liberation theologians, for they are criticized for attempting to describe the faith of poor peoples in manners that are foreign to that faith. They are also criticized for being disconnected from concrete faith communities within their countries.

## Critiques

The critiques of Latin American liberation theology emerging from numerous sectors of the Church and the academy are plentiful. These academic critiques are coupled with the decrease in the number of Latin Americans thinkers being translated into English. After all, as Elina Vuola thoughtfully points out, "it becomes more serious if new generations of scholars conclude from the lack of translations that 'if it does not exist in English, it does not exist,' and base their analysis on the meager and limited amount of translations."[28] This lack of access leads to an understanding of liberation theologies that is limited to the "classics" and offers little analysis of more recent writings. Is Latin American liberation theology dead, Vuola muses, because it is inaccessible to English-speaking audiences? Her point is the precise one for this study, which focuses on the U.S. academy. This dearth of translations into English is coupled with the accessibility in English of works by many of liberation theology's staunchest opponents.

There are various prominent voices of dissent against Latin American liberation theology. Often the collapse of European socialism and the fall of the Soviet Union are linked to Latin American liberation theology's demise, given that early liberation theologians' writings celebrated socialism. This link is perplexing, however, because scholars who cite it make a direct connection between an academic movement in Latin American and politics across the globe without even establishing a casual relationship between the two.[29] Vuola rightfully emphasizes that certain Latin American liberation theologians' praise for socialist Europe does not automatically equate European governments with the Latin American Church. Nonetheless, as Venezuelan sociologist Otto Maduro points out, the anticommunist persecutions in the 1960s through the 1980s and the death of liberationist activists in these persecutions contributed to the decline of liberationist movements in Latin America.[30] Often critiques point out that the Marxist emphasis on conflict within liberation theology stands in direct opposition to the Christian value of reconciliation and that the poor and oppressed are reduced to being a social class. Latin American liberation theology is accused of reducing faith to politics, uncritically using Marxism and praising socialism, and creating a separate church through the BCCs.

One of the greatest challenges to Latin American liberation theology has been the Vatican's offensive against it since the 1970s; this opposition has included attempts to silence key academic liberation theologians and to appoint people unsympathetic to liberation theology to key ecclesial positions.[31] In 1977, the International Theological Commission published an ambiguous dossier that both celebrated liberation theology and pointed out a perceived tension in the relationship between salvation and human works in this theology. At the 1979 CELAM conference in Puebla, Mexico, John Paul II seemed to simultaneously criticize Latin American liberation theology while affirming a concern for social justice.[32] The Congregation for the Doctrine of the Faith's 1984 *Instruction on Certain Aspects of the 'Theology of Liberation'* was a warning about certain deviations in liberation theology teachings. It also attacked liberation theology's Marxist assumptions and political ideologies.[33] The Vatican has also directly pursued theologians themselves, perhaps the most famous being Leonardo Boff. These moves are reinforced by the Vatican's support of movements such as Opus Dei, Focolarica, and the CCR. The overall strategy is to marginalize any liberationist impulses within the Latin American Church and to create a less-welcoming climate for liberation theologians.

The two major criticisms of Latin American liberation theology are its use of Marxist ideology and the creation of a popular church outside the official church.[34] These two themes surface repeatedly in various Christian contexts. The theological movement known as Radical Orthodoxy, which uses postmodern philosophy to critique modern secularism, has also weighed in with a substantial critique of Latin American liberation theologians. Perhaps best exemplified in the writings of theologian Daniel Bell, this critique accuses liberation theologians of surrendering to assumptions surrounding the capitalist construction of human rights and offering a limited understanding of the role of the Church. On the question of human rights he cites liberation theologians' emphasis on secular rights over a more communal understanding of the common good. Regarding the role of the Church, Bell writes, "They have acquiesced to the separation of religion from the socio-political-economic spheres of life, which entails depriving the Church of a forthright political presence, and have turned to the state as the principal agent of resistance to the capitalist order."[35] The Church, Bell argues, has become apolitical through the writings of Latin American liberation theologians and has been replaced by the state.

Joining the chorus of dissent is political theorist Paul E. Sigmund, who offers three critiques of liberation theology: its emphasis on a critique of capitalism, the assumption that the poor have a privileged window into religious enlightenment, and the rejection of liberalism.[36] For Sigmund, the romanticism of the poor and the construction of class conflict within liberation theology is a clear danger in Latin American writings. There is a difference, Sigmund argues, between presenting Christianity as a religion that has a concern for the marginalized and values solidarity with them versus arguing that the poor contain a special form of religious truth and the nonpoor must be defeated.[37] Sigmund's attack on Latin American liberation theologians' critique of capitalism is ironic, given a similar critique emerging from the Vatican through the Catholic Social Tradition.[38] He also presents a caricature that misrepresents the preferential option for the poor. Taking a different approach to the construction of the poor in liberation theology, anthropologist David Stoll argues that the radical nature of liberationist discourse is in fact alien to the very needs and worldview of the poor.[39] Both Sigmund and Stoll bring forth a significant challenge to Latin American thinkers. The construction of the poor in liberation theology should be problematized. The dualism of poor–nonpoor undercuts the complexity of the human person who cannot be reduced to merely economic class. Similarly, liberation theologians need to be accountable to their attribution of liberationist rhetoric to concrete poor peoples. The growth of evangelical Protestantism, with its deemphasis on political engagement, among poor Latin Americans clearly challenges the claim that politicized discourse is indeed organic to the poor.

Perhaps one of the most thoughtful responses to critiques of Latin American liberation theology is found in the scholarship of theologian David Tombs. Tombs acknowledges that liberation theology is currently in a state of crisis, asserting that, while this is not a moment of failure, it is one of transition.[40] In the 1990s, liberation theology faced new challenges: globalization, the rise of Pentecostalism, and lack of clear, unified political and economic analysis to replace dependency theory in light of the contemporary globalized economy.[41] As Tombs rightfully notes, all theological movements, especially ones that take seriously their sociohistorical context, share many of the challenges Latin American liberation theology faces.

> While liberation theology always had important limitations—and these certainly became more apparent in the 1990s—the same is true for any theological movement that engages with social issues on the historical plane. Liberation theology's terminology may now seem dated in the neo-liberal world economy, its social analysis often too limited and its theological foundations increasingly questionable, but the same criticism could be made of any other theology. None of liberation theology's difficulties in reading the signs of the times and presenting a prophetic response belong to liberation theology alone.[42]

Therefore many of the assaults launched at liberation theology in particular can be launched at all theologies in general. It is curious that Latin American and other liberation theologies have been principally under attack. One does not generally study Dietrich Bonhoeffer as passé due to the interconnection between his theological musings and his horror at the Nazi Party and its actions. Saint Augustine's *Confessions*, a classic in Christian theology, is not sidelined for its heavy contextual nature. The teachings of Vatican II are not seen as a relic of the 1960s. One might wonder, then, why theologies written by Latin Americans (and other Third World and U.S. minority peoples along with feminists) have been so heavily scrutinized for their contextual and historical limitations.

These attacks have led to the premature proclamations of the death of liberation theology. These premature obituaries are based on misunderstandings of the nature of liberation theology. Liberationist discourse has at times been alien to the worldview of poor people and has often been paternalistic. In a similar vein, liberation theology's heavy emphasis on social action in contrast to ritual and prayer has been foreign to the religiosity of the poor. This emphasis on the political has been at the expense of valuing daily life. "What needs to be buried is not liberation theology itself, but rather the exaggerated expectations and myths surrounding it.

Liberation theology has neither created protest and revolution (the myth of the Right), nor does it represent, much less organize, overwhelming popular majorities (the myth of the Left). With expectations of this magnitude, it is no wonder that hopes are disappointed: no one could fill this bill."[43] Linked to the high expectations placed on liberation theologians is unfamiliarity with the diversity and complexity that constitutes Latin American liberationist discourse. Perhaps what is unique about Latin American liberation theology is that for a brief time the institutional Church accompanied it in its struggles.[44] When that accompaniment waned, so did the theology in the eyes of many.

## Developments

In spite of the common practice of reading Gustavo Gutiérrez's *A Theology of Liberation* as if this book summarizes Latin American liberation theologies as a whole since the 1970s, there have been significant developments in this theological movement throughout the decades. Gutiérrez's work is a classic in Christian theology and a clear marker of the birth of this theological movement. However it does not embody Gutiérrez's corpus in particular and Latin American liberation theology in general. One has only to read books such as *We Drink from Our Own Wells* and *On Job: God-Talk and the Suffering of the Innocent*, to see a clear development in Gutiérrez's theology.[45] Within Latin American theology in general, Gutiérrez's contributions should be contextualized in light of the theological aesthetics of Rubem Alves and the postcolonial theology of Marcela Althaus-Reid, to name two among numerous distinct voices from Latin America.[46] This final section will focus on four areas of discussion and tension within Latin American theology that point to future avenues of development: popular/lived religion, the poor, religious pluralism, and theological method.

As a movement, Latin American liberation theology has experienced clear shifts in emphases, sources, and ideological framework. Sigmund marks several changes or points of development within Latin American

liberation theology over the decades. First is disenchantment with socialism and the expectation that the liberation of the poor will be widespread.
Instead, a more contextual, coalitional, grassroots understanding of liberation is now in place. Second, Latin American liberation theologians'
attitude toward Marxism is more nuanced than it was originally. Many
do not cite Marx in their contemporary research, and the romanticism of
European socialism has passed. Third, Sigmund argues, liberation theologians now have an awareness of the limitations of dependency theory.
Fourth, they embrace a more positive attitude toward democracy and
there has been a shift in the relationship with the institutional Church.
Fifth, one finds within the writings of Latin American liberation theologians an increased emphasis on spirituality.[47] These shifts in academic
liberation theology are a result, in part, of the ever-changing sociopolitical landscape over the past few decades. In addition, they reflect theologians' attempts to take into account a more comprehensive understanding of the faith of the poor, particular in light of their everyday religion.

## Popular Religion/Lived Religion

The disdain for popular religion among Latin American liberation theologians can be traced to the documents that emerged from the groundbreaking 1968 gathering of Latin American bishops in Medellín, where
bishops affirmed a commitment to the poor and marginalized. These
documents simultaneously acknowledged the significance of popular
religion while also calling for its study in order to "purify it of elements
that would make it inauthentic."[48] Yet, depicting Latin American liberation theology as, across the board, dismissive of popular religion is a
caricature at best. In his 1990 book, *Popular Religion and Liberation: The
Dilemma of Liberation Theology*, Michael Candelaria offers a synthesis
of the debate through a study of the theologies of Juan Carlos Scannone
(who considers popular religion a component of liberation) and Juan
Luis Segundo (who sees it as alienating).[49] Candelaria concludes with
his own constructive proposal, which is, in many ways, a synthesis of

the two opposing viewpoints. Those who oppose popular religion point to its fatalistic attitude, which legitimizes the status quo, for it keeps the focus of the poor on otherworldly salvation instead of on concrete social change. The other side argues for the liberating potential of popular religion because of its grassroots origin and its ability to mobilize social change.[50] Candelaria offers an interdisciplinary analysis of the topic and reveals the complexity of Latin American liberation theologians' views on the subject. He argues that popular religion and the popular church ought to be brought together as both the subject of truth and the object of critical academic study. The people are a source of truth, yet they must be intellectually guided.[51] His book also reveals that theological writings on popular religion began in Latin America in the 1970s and 1980s.[52]

In spite of the more complex view of popular religion articulated by Latin American liberation theologians, there is not a clear corpus of writings by them that specifically engages concrete practices. In other fields, however, the study of popular religion in Latin America is slowly growing. Scholar of religion Jennifer Scheper Hughes's study of the Cristo Aparecido, a crucifix that is the patron saint of the indigenous people in Totolapan, Mexico, offers "an exegesis of a specific, local Christian culture" that begins in 1548 and ends in the contemporary era.[53] Scheper Hughes combines the lived-religion approach with the study of local religion. "The emerging fields of 'lived' and 'local' religion represent a search for increasingly nuanced theoretical models and more satisfying interpretive frameworks for understanding what is traditionally termed, derided, and even disregarded as 'popular religion'—the faith, beliefs, and practices of poor, colonized, and marginalized people."[54] Her study also examines the manner in which the devotion encountered and was challenged by a liberation theology that often interpreted folk Christianity as an impediment to social transformation. Local religious practices were interpreted as vestiges of a colonial Spanish past. Scheper Hughes acknowledges that historically popular religious practices have served as tools of oppression that can lead to a spiritual passivity just as much as they can become means of political and social empowerment. Her study of the Cristo Aparecido demonstrates that pitting liberation theology against folk religion in Latin America is too simplistic an approach.

Latin American liberation theology promoted a modernist agenda while living side by side with the folk Catholicism that saturates the region. As an offspring of Vatican II, Latin American liberation theology is part of the Roman Catholic Church's broader project of modernization. Popular religion was seen as counter to the modernization project, not only by Latin America liberation theologians but also by the broader post-Vatican II Church, which sought to minimize devotionalisms, like folk saints. As a result, liberation theologians could not acritically embrace popular religion as a liberative dimension of Christian faith without examining its social, political, and theological import. Too often theological studies of popular religion gloss over the complex history and multilayered contemporary context in which these practices thrive. At times these practices perpetuate oppressive paradigms and social relationships. I witnessed this firsthand in the two years that I lived in a Mayan community in San Lucas Tolimán, Guatemala. Although the community had a rich and multilayered religious life centered on Roman Catholic feast days, I was shocked to encounter the rampant public alcoholism, violence, and debauchery that accompanied these Roman Catholic religious celebrations.

This complexity is also seen in the function of gender in popular religious practices. In her book, *Our Cry for Life: Feminist Theology from Latin America,* María Pilar Aquino touches on popular religion and its role in the lives of women as a sustainer of identity within everyday life.[55] Aquino focuses a critical eye on the motivations behind popular religion. For her, although popular religion is liberating, it also can be oppressive. In some ways, it has internalized "elements that legitimate submission to the oppressor."[56] Because it cannot be separated from culture, popular religion is a sustainer of identity and culture. It is part of one's heritage too. Aquino also reinforces the idea that popular religion is a sustainer of community through public rituals that engage the past, present, and future of communities. Aquino's broad claims cannot be applied to popular religion as a whole. Instead, such statements should be put in dialogue with concrete, sustained studies of particular practices.

The study of Latin American religion using a broad, interdisciplinary methodology is changing the landscape that Latin American liberation theologians inhabit. The book *Race, Nation, and Religion in the Americas*, edited by Henry Goldschmidt and Elizabeth McAlister, is a welcome addition to the study of religion in the Americas.[57] Appropriating a hemispheric approach, the book examines religion in North, South, and Central America and the Caribbean. The essays interweave historical studies with on-the-ground research of contemporary religious communities, often highlighting the intersection of history, culture, and politics. The book argues against the notion that in the contemporary world religion is no longer a significant component of community and identity. It would be incorrect to present the study of Latin American religion as exclusively theological.[58] This is but one path to academically accessing the religions of the poor.

### The Poor

Perhaps no phrase comes to mind more immediately than "the poor" when discussing the theological contribution of Latin American liberation theology. Yet, often liberation theologians have been accused of expressing a romanticized and acritical depiction of the poor that can render them spiritually naïve. The ability of academic theologians to authentically reflect the voice of the poor has become a key point of discussion and debate among liberation theologians. One critical assessment is Marcela Althaus-Reid's "indecent" theology, which she describes as a continuation and a disruption of liberation theology. She argues that liberation theology should engage in a "serious doubting" about the hermeneutical principles that have left it blind to the realities of the poor.[59]

Althaus-Reid maintains that the context from which liberation theology emerged in Latin America narrowed its focus so that it ignores the complexity of the poor, particularly with regard to gender and sexuality.

"Latin American liberation theology," she argues, "born out of an ethos of authoritarianism (social, political, and ecclesiastical), has missed the possibilities of theological *poiesis* that comes not from discourses on the idealized poor, but from the reality of the poor as people of different sexual and gender identities."[60] The idealized poor are those who fit into dominant theological and ecclesial models of social acceptability. Criticizing Latin American liberation theology's inability to get to know concrete poor individuals and how they live their lives, Althaus-Reid proclaims, "Liberation theology knows more about dogmas than about people."[61] Althaus Reid challenges Latin American liberation theologians to take gender and sexual identity seriously.[62] More broadly, however, she challenges the validity of claims that academic theologians make regarding the poor. Even when we record their stories and tape their narratives, the scholar is still present in the cultural construction of the marginalized. The question becomes, and this is for liberation theologians and scholars of lived religion, how can one give voice to the oppressed without controlling their voices?[63] Althaus-Reid challenges Latin American liberation theologians both to elaborate on how they are connected with the concrete realities of the poor people they claim to be writing about and to seriously reflect on how they approach the objects of their study. She reminds liberation theologians of the attitudes that they personally bring into their scholarship, attitudes that shape the manner in which the poor are interpreted and represented. A serious discussion of power and of how it functions in such relationships is needed. Also underlying this discussion is the question of accountability. How, in the end, are academic theologians accountable to the poor person they claim to represent in their books, articles, and presentations?

## Religious Pluralism and Christian Pluralism

A serious engagement with the concrete reality of poor peoples would reveal a far more complex religious world than is often found in the pages of Latin American liberation theologians' works. The broad Christian claims found in Latin American liberation theology are challenged by the presence of non-Christian religious elements, unofficial Christian practices, and a Christianity that is far more multifaceted than what is depicted by liberation theologians. A case study for this complexity is the devotional life dedicated to folk saints in Latin America. Frank Graziano explores national cults developed around folk saints in Argentina, Mexico, and Peru.[64] What are folk saints? They are often referred to in Spanish as *santos populares* or *santos paganos*. Sometimes a folk saint is a deceased person who is believed to be miraculous and around whom has developed a large cult that is not recognized or canonized by the Catholic Church. These cults expand to countries other than those that Graziano outlines in his work, including to the United States.

Graziano emphasizes that most of the devotees to these saints are Catholic, which begs the question: Why do they venerate them and not canonized saints? Graziano offers a few theories. For many, folk saints are more miraculous. Because the official Church has rejected some, their healing and transformative power transcends the institution of the Catholic Church. A second factor is that of *lo nuestro*, what is ours or belonging to us. The folk saint becomes a transcendent extension of the devotees, their communities, and their culture. A third factor is the flawed humanity of folk saints. For example, if one needs help in stealing one cannot ask an official saint, but a folk saint, who is imperfect, who may have transgressed, might intercede. A fourth factor is the locality of the folk saint: other saints are very busy, but a folk saint addresses or gives priority only to his or her community. A final factor is the freedom of devotion. There is no dogma between devotee and folk saint. An expression Graziano encountered in his ethnographic research is *hay que creer en algo*, looking for something that is one's own after loss of faith in institutionalized religion.

How do you become a folk saint? In the cases studied by Graziano, many suffered a tragic death. This economy of atonement leads to an understanding of tragic death that cleanses your sins because you have suffered so much. *Curandero/as,* or faith healers, can also be sanctified as folk saints. Believers may be in desperate need of a miracle (there is an emergency, they are chronically ill, they have exhausted other resources). Often they enter into a spiritual contract with the folk saint. Interactions may include petitions and promises: "If you do this . . . I will do this," known as *pagar una manda*. If you do not do what you promised, the folk saint will punish you; there is reciprocity to the relationship. Or believers may ask a folk saint for protection.

The relationship between folk devotion and the institutional Catholic Church is not always clear. The policies that churches have vary wildly by parish priest and local bishop: some are tolerant, others are not. It is significant that devotees often do not distinguish between official and folk devotions. When a priest does not support devotion to a folk saint, the people are offended. Devotion to folk saints opens up the issue of the non-Christian within Latin American liberation theology.[65] The presence of non-Christians challenges not only the content or focus of the study of religion but also the methodology. Yet the non-Christian is present within Christianity. The discipline of religious studies has defined and approached religion through a Western Christian framework. This theism leads to a dualistic understanding of the sacred and the profane. This sentiment is echoed by the classic formulation of Asian liberation theologian Aloysius Pieris, who reminds us that "the vast majority of God's poor perceive their ultimate concern and symbolize their struggle for liberation in the idiom of non-Christian religions and cultures."[66] The religion of the non-Christian poor must become a point of discussion for the future of liberation theologies.

## Method versus Theocentrism

Latin American liberation theologians are often heralded for the methodological revolution they initiated in the study of theology. And, yet, was the intention really methodological or was it theocentric? Liberation theologies understand poverty as scandalous to God, for God wants all of God's creation to have dignity and to flourish. In situations of oppression, God is not neutral. This preferential option for the poor is due to the situation of oppression. The poor are in no way closer to God or holier per se, yet their context demands liberation: "The purpose of this divine partiality is to heal, redeem, and liberate the situation so that the dehumanizing suffering will cease."[67] The preferential option for the poor emerges from the conviction that, as oppressed and alienated, the poor will offer a vision of hope that counters and overcomes these conditions, for while forgotten by us they are embraced by God.[68] Latin American theologians ground their insights in the Hebrew and Christian Scriptures, arguing that they reveal a God on the side of the oppressed.

In addition to revealing something about God taking sides, Latin American liberation theologians argue that the poor reveal something about God's presence. "The existence of the poor attests to the existence of a Godless society, whether one explicitly believes in God or not. This absence of God is present when someone is crying out. The absence of God is present in the poor person. The poor are the presence of the absent God."[69] The poor reveal the Christian God and, as such, reveal the nature of God. Latin American liberation theology is a theology of orthopraxis, not orthodoxy; it emphasizes right action versus right belief, a well-known claim by many liberation theologians. The methodological claim, however, seems to emerge from the theological claim about the nature of the Christian God. A society that struggles against oppression reveals God's presence.

The theocentric emphasis of Latin American liberation theology is found in the work of Gutiérrez, whose method became increasingly theocentric as his theology progressed. God is the God of life and has a preferential option for the poor.[70] One is called to opt for the poor because God has opted for the poor. This theocentric emphasis is echoed by Latin American liberation theologian Pablo Richard when he writes, "The theology of liberation is not a theological reflection on liberation, but rather a reflection on God in a context of liberation."[71] His claims about liberation are grounded theologically in his concept of the sacred.

It is not social theory that informs the preferential option for the poor; it is God who demands this option of us.

An emphasis on the theological versus methodological focus of Latin American liberation theology would also move scholars away from eulogies that announce its demise based on the collapse of socialism and dependency theory. Althaus-Reid has continuously challenged liberation theologians to recognize how their writings have been tamed and domesticated by the Western theological academy.[72] What is truly transgressive about Latin American liberation theology is not its methodology, is not its use of social sciences or its emphasis on Christian praxis. What is truly subversive and challenging about Latin American liberation theology is the claims it makes about God, about the essence of the sacred and how God acts in human history, transforming the very nature of the Christian religion. Latin American liberation theology does not need to move on to other topics. Latin American liberation theology should not abandon its primary commitments, yet today it is challenged to find new methods and new language to speak of and for the faith and struggles of the Latin American poor in light of the broader issues of social justice that are prevalent throughout the Americas.

2

# Black Liberation Theology

Black liberation theology exploded into the theological arena in the late 1960s with a fervor that ignited the North American and later international theological communities. It emerged at the same historical moment as Latin American liberation theology, and together these theologies represent a shift in the method and sources of theology. Black liberation theologians introduced the category of race into theological speculation, demonstrating the manner in which historical and contemporary Christianity supports and perpetuates racist paradigms. Although black liberation theologians are not the first to write about the religion of African Americans, they are the first to explicitly engage academic theology.

Black liberation theologians argue that, for centuries, religion has been used to legitimize discrimination in the United States. In their early years, black liberation theologians argued that the African American response was a refusal to accept this interpretation of Christianity. Slaves transformed the religion imposed on them into a liberative Christianity. The religion of the slave master became the religion of the slaves, and the Exodus account of the Hebrew liberation from Egyptian slavery became paradigmatic for black liberation theologians' theistic claims about the nature of God. Black theologians have historically grounded such claims through studies of the spirituals, slave narratives, and slave religion. They understand the collectivity of black Protestant churches, categorized by scholars as the Black Church, as embodying this liberationist impulse. In recent years this depiction of black Christianity has been nuanced. Scholars of African American religion have challenged these simplistic claims about the historical religion of slaves and the more recent history of the Black Church. The history of African American churches in the United States is not entirely one of social justice and liberation, but an internalized spirituality has been a strong focus. During the civil rights movement, justice emerged as central to African American Christianity, yet it is not pervasive in all African American churches.[1]

The category of black liberation theology emerged in the late 1960s on both ecclesial and academic fronts through the Statement by the National Committee of Black Churchmen on July 31, 1966, and the publication of James H. Cone's *Black Theology and Black Power*.[2] The ecclesial and academic roots of this theology are significant. Because of its dual origins, black liberation theology has struggled to define its audience and to find a way to translate academic insights into the ecclesial realm. Similarly, although in its first years academic black liberation theology was connected to black churches, as the decades have passed it has become increasingly disconnected from everyday Christians. Within the academy, the first generation of black theologians was criticized by later generations for their limited understanding of black experience.

A significant critique emerges from feminist black theologians who adopted writer Alice Walker's definition of *womanist* to name their collective theological voices.[3] Womanist theology responds to the dualism of black women and white women or black women and black men, challenging feminist theologians to take race seriously in their theological analysis and black theologians to take gender analysis seriously in their theological work. The discourse of womanist theology must be situated within the development of critical black feminism. Womanism is something to which black women choose to adhere; it is not imposed on them. Its sources include black women's lived experience and literature. Womanist theology is multidialogistic, liturgical, pedagogical, and theological. It utilizes a tripartite analysis that examines the dynamics of racism, sexism, and classism in African-American women's lives. Black women's culture is a primary resource for womanist theology, with a strong emphasis on narrative through the recovery of black women's texts. In retrieving these narrative texts womanist theologians highlight black women's creativity in the midst of oppression. A strong emphasis is placed on God as Spirit and its presence in culture and creation.[4] Within womanist theology, black women's experiences are interpreted through cultural codes. However, not all cultural activity is life-affirming. Womanist theologians call for a multiplicity of symbols surrounding the sacred and emphasize the limits of human constructions.

Womanists are not the only theologians who have engaged the first generation of black liberation theologians in a critique of their essentialist claims regarding African American Christianity in the United States. As the study of African American religion has grown in the U.S. academy, new methodologies have expanded and critiqued this first generation of scholars. Yet many of these scholars return to the prophetic African American religion of the 1960s, which fuels their interpretations of liberationist impulses within black religion. Those eyes that keep gazing toward the past must turn and look at the present and future of black theology today.

Theologians are not the only scholars doing substantial work on African American religion. The field of African American religious studies offers an alternative approach that at times complements and at others challenges the prominence of theology within the study of black religion. This chapter explores the impact of the scholars working on black religion since the 1960s with an eye to the future of the field, drawing from both black theologians and black scholars working in African American religious studies.

## Defining Black Religion

Although black liberation theologians are not the first to write about African American religious experience, their impact on the field of

African American religion is profound. Black theologians delineated the study of African American religion as exclusively Christian and primarily ecclesial. The influence of Cone, not only through his publications but also through his mentoring of African American doctoral students, produced a generation of scholars heavily influenced by his Christian theological approach, which grounded black liberation theology in the civil rights and black power movements. This definition of black religion was rooted in black churches and a depiction of them as justice-infused and redefining Christianity as a religion of the oppressed whose ultimate goal was liberation. Naming Jesus as black and God as black recast Christianity as a religion in which the Christian God, as interpreted through the ministry, teachings, and suffering of Jesus, is ultimately and exclusively on the side of the oppressed.

> Christ's blackness is both literal and symbolic. His blackness is literal in the sense that he truly becomes One with the oppressed blacks, taking their suffering as his suffering and revealing that he is found in the history of our struggle, the story of our pain, and the rhythm of our bodies. . . . To say Christ is black means that black people are God's poor people whom Christ has come to liberate. . . . Christ is black, therefore, not because of some cultural or psychological need of black people, but because and only because Christ *really* enters into our world where the poor, the despised, and the black are, disclosing that he is with them, enduring their humiliation and pain and transforming oppressed slaves into liberated servants.[5]

Jesus as the black Christ identifies with black suffering and liberation. Jesus (and God's) blackness is symbolic, pointing to suffering and humiliation in need of liberation.[6] For Cone blackness symbolizes oppression, and race is the most appropriate lens through which to understand Jesus's solidarity with the oppressed. Roman Catholic theologian M. Shawn Copeland challenges this construction of the sacred when she argues that poverty, not race, is the entry point for understanding the sacred: "Poor is the color of God because God has made the liberation of poor, excluded, and despised persons a divine goal. To say that poor is the color of God is to say that God has made the condition of the poor, excluded and despised, God's own."[7] She grounds her claim in Scripture and in Jesus's assuming the condition of poverty during his historical life. Poverty is also inclusive of race, particularly when one examines the demographics of the poor in the United States. Ultimately both Cone and Copeland share an emphasis on oppression. Although perspectives like Copeland's expand the understanding of the sacred, the predominance of race marks the discourse of black theology.

The foundation of black liberation theology is the religious experience of African Americans, often exclusively defined as African American experiences of Christianity.[8] Slave religion is a primary historical source, from which a liberationist reading of slave religion depicts the transformation of Christianity from the religion of the oppressor to the religion of the oppressed. The bible also plays a significant role, particularly liberationist interpretations of the Hebrew Scriptures and Christian Scriptures. African American churches, collectively categorized as the Black Church, become a central site for the expression of black liberationist Christianity. Radical politics and struggles for liberation, particularly in light of the activism of the 1960s, are benchmarks of liberationist Christian praxis. In addition, the broad and unclear category of black experience also plays a central role within black and womanist theologies. The sources of this experience include cultural production, narrative, music, and literature.

The inclusion of cultural production reveals a point of tension within the scholarship of black theologians, who often viewed political engagement as being at odds with an emphasis on culture. This view mirrors the discussion of Latin American liberation theology about the role of popular religion. Given Cone's influence, his political interpretation of African American Christianity was definitive for the early decades of black liberation theology. Cone emphasizes political liberation from U.S. white racism as fundamental to the work of black liberation theologians.

This salvation is not passive but instead involves active participation in the struggle against oppression.

Cone's approach is not the only path within black liberation theology. Theological scholars such as black theologian, ethicist, and historian Gayraud Wilmore strive to broaden the sources and method of black theology in order to address the totality of African American religious experiences. Wilmore understands liberation as more than political and sees culture as a vehicle of liberation. His scholarship emphasizes folk religion, traditional African religion, and sermons. Historian of religion Charles Long also calls for a cultural approach to African American religion, one that explores African Americans' experience of the holy outside of the ecclesial setting. In addition to being critical of the manner in which black theology is wedded to churches, Long is suspicious of the very discipline of theology. For Long, theology is too interlaced with whites, and the language of theology is inappropriate for African Americans because of its imperialistic roots.

Long's critique of the over-ecclesial nature of black liberation theology is one that has resonated with scholars of black theology and African American religious experience. The role of the Black Church and its role in black liberation theology remain contested themes among scholars of African American religion. A substantial critique claims that black theology is too tied to black churches. This viewpoint is seen in the work of humanist theologian Anthony Pinn and of philosopher of religion Victor Anderson.[9] Both challenge the centrality of the Black Church, noting that when black religion becomes equated with the Black Church, religion is not open to hard questioning.

Not only is the emphasis on black churches problematic, but so is the relationship between black theology and black churches. Few black churches are aware of academic black theology.[10] Black liberation theologians are criticized for their lack of connection with everyday African American Christians. In addition, their scholarship does not reflect a systematic engagement with concrete ecclesial communities; nor is there a sense of reception and expression of black liberation theology within

African American churches. Part of this estrangement is based on a class distinction in which the liberationist thrust of black theologians is alien to many evangelical and liberal churches. Black liberation theology has a strained relationship with black churches and black culture. This distance is experienced not only by black theologians but also by black churches. Anderson questions what black churches have down on behalf of marginalized African American communities. Although not wanting to discard heroic depictions of the Black Church and perhaps not going so far as to state that black churches need to promote academic black theology, Anderson questions what they are doing for the black community today to combat systemic racism.[11]

African American religion has been constructed theistically by black theologians and is often synonymous with the Black Church. Within black liberation theology African American religion has been given a privileged status and is therefore not open to critical questioning. As the great sustainer of African American identity, as the constructed advocate of the oppressed, the Black Church often enjoys theologians' acritical stance toward it. Womanist theologians have begun to question the glorification of the Black Church particularly in light of sexism. In addition to these critiques there is an awareness that the current construction of historical black religion is based on limited knowledge of the past. Too often black theologians have imposed a construction of present liberationist trends and read it into historical African American religious practices. Cultural anthropologist Marla Frederick notes that the polarities of radicalism and liberation limit the complexity of the ecclesial life and everyday faith of African Americans.[12] Not every form of resistance needs to be a political protest. Frederick emphasizes, for example, that not all black churches supported the civil rights movement and notes the manner in which the Black Church limits women's agency. Because creation implies agency, creativity is a form of resistance; resistance should not be reduced just to political agency.

The complexity of historical recovery has been central to the scholarship of Anderson, who is critical of the slave-narrative project within black liberation theology.[13] The defenders of this project (theologians Dwight Hopkins, George Cummings, Will Coleman, and Cheryl Sanders) hold that slave narratives are representative of slave religiosity and culture. Anderson argues that there is too strong a correlation between the slave narratives and contemporary black theology: "The slave narratives are rendered as just so much *proto-black liberation theology*. At its best, this is an anachronism, and at its worst, this is hermeneutical violence for the sake of reassuring the identity of the black theology project by grounding it in authentic African American religious experience."[14] Slave religion does not equal the slave narratives, which reveal only one dimension of religious practices. Anderson reminds us that African America religion is opaque, although not in a negative sense. The opacity or ambiguity of historical memory regarding historical African American religion must be respected, and it should not be rendered transparent. Scholars have to hold onto the ambiguity of black religious life. The Western European discourse of theology often does not allow for the ambiguities of black religious experience, wanting clear and systematic answers.

Another layer of this discussion pertains to blackness within black theology. Does black equal African American? What about non-African American U.S. blacks? Roman Catholic theologian Diana Hayes broadens the category of peoples of African descent to include people from Latin America and the Caribbean. Building on the work of Mexican educator and philosopher José Vasconcelos, Hayes presents a vision of a new people, one constituted by racial mixture.[15] In a similar vein, ethicist Marcia Riggs calls for a "cross-racial and cross-cultural kaleidoscope" that highlights racial and ethnic diversity.[16] Riggs provocatively states, "African Americans seem unable (unwilling?) to relinquish their status as the most beleaguered minority in the United States."[17] This stance leads to the polarization of African Americans and other marginalized communities. They are trapped in this polarity. Riggs also emphasizes that this belief limits African American engagement on issues of same-sex marriage, public education, and immigration. The case of immigration becomes a competition arena. She argues for an expanded notion of justice that broadens the moral community of African Americans and cultivates empathy and reconciliation.

Both Hayes and Riggs raise the question, Who are the subjects of black theology? Although many scholars of black theology tend to speak of the Black Church and black religious experience as though their research addresses blacks as a whole, what they actually mean is Christian (overwhelmingly Protestant) African American religious experience. Black theologians use African American and black interchangeably in a manner that negates the diversity of black religion in the United States. They also, explicitly and implicitly, exclude blacks who do not share African American religious experience—for example, Caribbean blacks and Afro-Latins—from their scholarship. This exclusion creates a narrow definition of black religion within black theology, one that does not engage the complexity of black religious life.

In his groundbreaking work on the plurality of African American experiences, Pinn argues that a much broader range of religions than black Christianity constitutes African American religious experience. African American theologians, for the most part, have ignored non-Christian religions in their writings, limiting the nature and scope of their work. These sources include Yoruba religion, Voodoo, the Nation of Islam, and humanism. The centrality of Christianity makes Christian doctrine and concerns normative for African American religiosity. Theology must address religious experience without limiting itself to one religious tradition. Non-Christian religions cannot be seen as supplementing Christian faith but must be seen as contributing to a broader understanding of African American religion. Resonating with Anderson's comments, Pinn highlights the fragility and fragmentation black religious experiences. Pinn calls for a "theology of fragile memory and religious diversity."[18] This theological method would function by defining one's issues and sites of study, doing research on these sites, proposing some initial theories, recording one's research, and analyzing it theologically. Concrete, on-the-ground scholarship must inform one's definition of black religion.

An example of such research is found in African American historian Anthea Butler's study of the role of women in the Church of God
in Christ. Her work examines the role of the church mothers within a
particular Pentecostal church as spiritual mothers and matriarchal leaders.[19] Butler argues that her work is a corrective in African American
ecclesial studies in that it looks at a church in transition. Butler contests
the rigid constructions of the Black Church operative within ecclesial
studies, claiming they ignore the subtle and complex ways in which religion functions in civic life. Hers is a more fluid understanding of a black
church based on ethnography and historical research. The combination
allows for the opacity, in the words of Anderson, to be maintained within
the study of African American religion.

At the root of the role of the Black Church is the role of theology.
Most theologians assume that the theistic nature of their enterprise is
exclusively Christian. This has led to the supposition that Christianity
is the most significant and authentic form of religious expression for
African Americans.[20] I do not contest the significance of Christianity
for understanding African American religion. However, it is only one
piece, albeit a significant one, of a larger narrative about black religion.
Studies of African American folk healing, for example, reveal a complex
religious world. Folk healing informs African American identity, culture,
and religion. It is both a communal and an individual practice that is
found in African American religious life, art, social activism, and relationships.[21] Exploring the fullness and complexity of African American
religion requires a much broader definition than has been provided by
black theologians.

In the end, however, the Black Church is a central dimension of
African American religious experience: "The church is not just about
redemption, it is also about pain and subjugation. In spite of the pain,
black churches are on par with the beauty shop as one of the few venues
in America where African American women can congregate together,
focusing their hopes and dreams on bettering themselves, their children,
their men, and their world."[22] Yet the Black Church is far more complex

than it has been depicted, and many black churches today do not fit the paradigm that has been constructed by black theologians. In fact, some never did. In addition, the Black Church must be understood in light of the complexity and diversity of African American religion. Non-Christian religions cannot simply be add-ons to a Christian framework. The manner in which black theology and African American religious studies define black religion is explicitly connected to the method that scholars use. Questions of content are intimately linked to questions of approach.

## Approach

The primacy of theology within the study of African American religion is being challenged on various fronts. Since its inception, black liberation theology has been a contested form of discourse from within the theological field. Although James Cone is a foundational voice in black theology, even his earliest writings did not go unchallenged. Both Wilmore and Cecil Cone criticized the perceived Eurocentrism of his scholarship, which they felt relied too heavily on European theologians, particularly the work of Karl Barth. Underlying their critique was the need for black theology to draw more heavily from African American sources and not to become dominated by the agenda of traditional European and Euro-American theology. This view resonates with Long's concerns regarding the imperialistic nature of theology as a whole. Yet another challenge raised by Long is focused on the originality of black liberation theology's initial claims. Long argues that many of Cone's key insights— for example, seeing Jesus and God as black,—are not original. What is original to Cone's writings are their location within systematic theology.[23]

Theologian William Jones's book, *Is God a White Racist? A Preamble to Black Theology*, challenges the assumption that God is on the side of the oppressed given their continued suffering.[24] He instead proposes a "humanocentric theism" that deemphasizes God's work in theodicy and instead places accountability in human hands. The question of divine racism has been ignored by black theologians. Cone, Jones argues, creates a discourse in which one must refute the notion of divine racism in black theology. Why are blacks oppressed in spite of God's favor? Don't we need to explain how their plight began in the first place? If Christianity has been saturated with racism, then the tradition needs to be heavily scrutinized. How much should be thrown out? Cone claims that God's nature is mediated only through liberation on the side of the oppressed. In addition, black theologians often rely on an eschatological construction of black suffering that is problematic. How can we confirm that God's activity will be different in the future? Black theologians do not sufficiently legitimate this eschatological end to black suffering in the hands of God. Although I agree that the concept of a benevolent God on the side of the oppressed is an authentic understanding of the Christian God, the "why" surrounding the brutal historical suffering of black peoples remains. What justifies such suffering? Linked to this question is the heavy emphasis on redemptive suffering within black theology, which is explored in the final section of this chapter.

Jones's critique could be applied to liberation theologies as a whole, for the notion of God's liberative preferential option for the oppressed is challenged by the brutal and dehumanizing suffering of marginalized peoples throughout history. If it is their condition of oppression that makes them privileged, then what does this reveal about the nature of God? Does God need the oppressed to suffer? The question of the privileging of historically oppressed peoples begs the question of the nature of a God who seems to somehow need human suffering. Such privileging could be easily misconstrued when connected to the human suffering of Jesus on the cross, as if the God of Christianity demands such suffering as a path to redemption. I do not disagree with Cone's claim that "black faith emerged out of black people's wrestling with suffering, the struggle to make sense out of their senseless situation, as they related their own predicament to similar stories in the Bible."[25] However, I also do not think that this process leads to a theocentric vision of the Christian God as a God that condemns suffering. As Jones's critique rightfully points out, the Christian narrative is much more complex.

Although there have been second- and third-generation developments of black theology, both share similar qualities in that they accepted the inherited paradigm of the first generation of black theologians. Yet, today, a shift appears at hand, one in which more and more scholars who work on African American religious studies (instead of theology) are changing the focus of the field. In addition, scholars who remain within the theological discipline are broadening their sources and conversation partners. Interdisciplinary work in postmodern, postcolonial, and cultural studies demonstrates that black theology is not an isolated endeavor, although more needs to be done in these areas. The construction of blackness within black liberation theology has been contested by numerous scholars.[26] Womanist theology has also been challenged for its use of the category of womanist, both misappropriating Walker's definition and creating an uncritical definition of black women's experience.[27] These challenges do not hail the death of theology but perhaps do imply the death of a certain type of theology, one that is too wedded to a theological approach that was appropriate in the 1960s and 1970s but no longer resonates today.

Within black theology the role of European and Euro-American theology has become a point of contention. One approach emphasizes the need to recover black sources exclusively within black theology, but other scholars directly engage traditional theology as a conversation partner within their work. At the heart of ethicist Bryan Massingale's *Racial Justice and the Catholic Church* is an exploration of the relevance of the Roman Catholic faith for the struggle for racial justice in the present-day United States.[28] The book has a twofold focus: demonstrating how a Catholic method of approaching racial justice can be significant for us today and demonstrating how an emphasis on racial justice can challenge and develop Catholic social ethics. While acknowledging the presence of a Catholic voice on this topic, Massingale points to the lack of social analysis in the Church's reflection on racism. Even more challenging is the claim Massingale makes that the U.S. Church is a white-racist institution in which whiteness is normative for U.S. Catholicism. Drawing from the broader Christian tradition, Massingale suggests Catholics' renewed engagement with racial reconciliation. Ultimately, however, if Catholics do not understand racism as a force in direct conflict with their faith they will never become active in the struggle against racial injustice. Although some black theologians will critique Massingale's heavy emphasis on the dominant theological tradition, it forces the question of the relevance of black theology beyond traditional black churches and the African American community.

Increasingly scholars who self-define as researching African American religion explicitly reject the primacy of theology as the most appropriate approach to black religion. The 2003 publication of *African American Religious Thought: An Anthology*, edited by Cornel West and Eddie S. Glaude Jr., was a pivotal moment in the field.[29] While acknowledging the groundbreaking work of black theology, this introduction calls for new questions to be asked and new approaches to be taken within the field of African American religious studies. Black theology has led to a legacy of theological commitments that have become definitive for the field, even within attempts to define African American religious studies in a more interdisciplinary manner. This significant anthology marks a paradigm shift: "What we have set out to do in this massive undertaking is offer a new direction for the field. We do not hold the view that theological education frames the entire enterprise of African American religious studies. It is simply one crucial yet distinct part of a differentiated field of inquiry."[30] Black religious studies needs to emphasize black religious expressions in all their complexities. The editors argue that black religion cannot be reduced to one religion or religious institution. Their use of the term strives to encompass the diversity of beliefs, practices, and institutions that constitute black religion. The role of the scholar of African American religion is to critically engage understandings of black religion. The book contains several historical studies and frames the field within black religious history, black theology, and the sociology of black religion.

Challenging the primacy of theology is not merely an academic quibble over whose approach is most appropriate for understanding African

American religion. At the root of this debate is how best to address the challenges not exclusively posed by black theologians but by African American religion as a whole. It is clear that black theology has not been effective in its transmission to a broader audience beyond the academy. Of course, one could state this is an unfair critique of black theology as an academic discipline, one that is not raised with other forms of academic theology. However, black theology claims that it emerges from grassroots Christian churches. It states that the ecclesial setting is in part its audience. And on that point black theology has fallen short, not because of unfair expectations emerging from the outside but because of the expectations it delineated for itself. Also in question is the role of African American Christian churches as authoritative within black theology. The role of ecclesial authority is not often explored within the pages of black theology.

Wilmore highlights five factors that contribute to black theology's inability to reach its full potential: the lack of infrastructure to engage the ecclesial context; the rise of conservative, charismatic black religiosity in the 1970s and 1980s; the death of the Honorable Elijah Muhammad in 1975; the Nixon administration's elimination of black radicals and emphasis on black capitalism; and the lukewarm reception of black theology by the white academy. One has the impression reading his work that black theology has been in decline since the early 1980s. The shifts Wilmore highlights are significant, for they demonstrate that perhaps black liberation theologians have become out of touch with their current religious context and instead rely too heavily on an African American Christianity of the past. A question that also emerges from Wilmore's analysis is whether black liberation theology should remain wedded to the theologian's theological vision regarding what is authentic, liberative Christianity or whether it is required to explore Christian expressions that do not fall into the paradigm of established liberationist African American Christianity. This question becomes most pressing in light of the conservative and evangelical black Christianity that is on the rise. Theologian James Evans also highlights the challenges posed by new religious movements, such as prosperity gospel, for contemporary black theology.[31] A God that promotes wealth is radically different from the God of the oppressed within liberation theologies.

Wilmore never had grand expectations about a massive movement emerging around black theology because none had emerged in the twentieth century from other intellectual Christian movements. Black theology remained too much of a middle-class, intellectual movement and hampered the ability of black scholars of religion to connect with everyday African Americans: "Most of us have become so old, middle-class, tenured, and disoriented by personal greed and the irresponsible use of power, that we have permitted the radical tradition in African American culture and religion to become weakened and trivialized."[32] Black theology has been unable to translate itself to youth, churches, and schools. Unless black theologians open themselves up to broader audiences and interdisciplinary research, they will continue to isolate themselves within not only the general academy but also the broader public.

## Audience

Linked to the discussion of methodology and content (the how and what of black theology) is the question of audience. Black liberation theologians claim it to be a theology that engages both the church and the academy, nourished and tested by both. Yet the effectiveness of their scholarship in both realms has been contested. In addition, African American scholars in the field of religious studies challenge black theologians to engage the broader public. Black theology has not been a successful public theology outside the halls of the academy. In light of these concerns, the intended audience of black theology today is a significant point of discussion.

The "failure" of black theologians to engage a broader audience beyond the academy must be contextualized in light of the study of Christianity as a whole. Prophetic Christian philosopher Cornel West situates the study of African American religion within a religious life in the United States that has lost its prophetic edge. He sees this loss not only in academic circles but also in lived religious contexts (and not exclusively Christian ones).[33] The religious intellectual is in a particular bind, for he or she must navigate the tension of the modern world and the weight of historical religious traditions. West describes the definitive feature of Christianity today as its mediocrity: there is no great thinker or prophet.[34] He blames the current situation on two factors: the cowardice of Euro-American theology and the superficial acceptance of liberation theology. It all stems, he argues, from Christian thinkers' inability to adequately respond to the 1960s. In addition, with a few notable exceptions, an American theology has not been developed, and, instead, the uncritical turn to European sources. West, in a sense, is lamenting the demise of grassroots activist Christianity broadly conceived. For black theologians, the question becomes one of sources. What happens if the activist African American Christianity of the 1960s no longer exists? What becomes the main source for black liberation theology? Is it the theological commitments of the author or a romanticized nostalgia for a Christian past? An additional factor is the complexity of the black community today. The diversity of the black community throughout the Americas should be a central topic of discussion for black theologians. The black community cannot be reduced to the African American community. Black oppression cannot be reduced to race. I am not denying that racism still exists; however, blanket statements about the African American as homogenously oppressed no longer ring true today.

The question of audience is deeply connected to the formation of black theologians. West provides theologians with a critique of the religious, intellectual, and moral landscape of the United States: "Our seminaries and divinity schools are not only simply in intellectual disarray and existential disorientation; our very conception of what they should be doing are in shambles."[35] Theological centers of education operate with the double-consciousness of the academy and the church. However, they do not sufficiently address the question of what relevance the academy has to everyday Christians. Theological curricula need to be revised in light of these concerns. One cannot study theology geared toward churches and theology and religious studies geared toward the academy in the same manner. This is a broader concern that expands beyond the field of black theology, but nonetheless it is significant for the audience and the impact of black theologians given the rootedness of black theology in Christian seminaries and divinity schools. This concern also concretizes the claim in this book that the issues raised by examining liberation theologies are broad issues for the religion academy as a whole.

Many of these concerns are not foreign to the scholarship of black theologians. The question of black theology's accessibility to the poor and within ecclesial settings is a thread we see in numerous writings. It is also one that has an impact on both Latino/a and Latin American theologies. Uniting these theologies is a claimed commitment to and engagement with grassroots churches. However, all these theologies have struggled to find a way concretely to engage churches in a sustained way. In addition, these theologies suffer from a bi-locality within the academy and the church that has not been sufficiently explored. One cannot write to the academy in the same way one writes to the church. Unfortunately, being scholars in academic institutions, most theologians overwhelmingly and exclusively write for the academy.

Even within the academic realm black theologians have been limited in their conversations outside the discipline of theology. Black theologians have been active in the Ecumenical Association of Third World Theologians (EATWOT) since the late 1970s. Here, black theologians challenged the category of "Third World," arguing that racial ethnic minorities in the United States may live in a First World country, but they live under Third World conditions. Black theologians also have dialogued explicitly with African theologians, focusing on their commonalities of shared ancestry and a common struggle against white supremacy. They have also engaged Latin American liberation theologians on the question of class and how race functions within the Latin American context. Increasingly there are collaborations with U.S. minority theologians. Womanist theologians have always sustained a dialogue with other feminist theologians. All these conversations are significant. Yet they all occur exclusively within the theological academy.

A key piece missing in these exchanges is explicit and intentional conversations with scholars who embrace a religious studies approach to the study of African American religion. Too often, black theologians isolate themselves among other theologians and do not have important conversations about method, the primacy of Christianity, and the construction of the Black Church. I am not arguing that to engage religious studies will save black theology from its limitations. I am certain, however, that if this methodological cross-fertilization does not occur black theology will continue to become increasingly irrelevant within the academy and within Christian churches. It is ironic that several scholars who work within African American religious studies have conducted concrete studies of black churches (Butler and Frederick come to mind), yet these scholars neither claim a glorified understanding of how their research affects the church nor do they claim that their scholarship defines black Christianity as a whole. Collaborations among scholars of a variety of methodologies will strengthen the study of African American religion, regardless of an individual scholar's methodological orientation.

In addition to broadening its methodological conversation partners, black theology has to find a way to translate itself into the political realm through the creation of think tanks, publishers, and policy institutes: "Black theology needs to establish a strategic presence at the places where political and economic decisions are made and—perhaps even more important, to indicate to blacks, whites, and other ethnic minorities, the points at which theological and spiritual questions intersect with public issues."[36] In other words, black theology needs to become a more public theology. The 2008 presidential elections were one moment when controversy allowed theologians to enter into the public arena. Misunderstandings of the theology of Jeremiah Wright and Barack Obama's connections to his Trinity United Church of Christ in Chicago created a teaching moment in which black theologians were able to have a public forum to explain their theological perspectives. However, theologians cannot sit and wait for another controversy in order to find their public voice.

Entering into a more public discourse, however, requires an assessment of the complex relationship between black religion and politics. The complexity of black religion cannot be erased. Broad generalizations about "the Black Church" and "African American Christianity" are no longer useful and were never true in the totalizing manner academics have used these terms. As Barbara Savage reminds us, "Despite common usage, there is no such thing as the 'black church.' It is an illusion and a metaphor that has taken on a life of its own, implying the existence of a powerful entity of organized power, but the promise of that also leaves it vulnerable to unrealistic expectations."[37] In addition, the myth born during the civil rights movement that black Christianity and politics were aligned has been rightfully contested. Nonetheless, given the historical and contemporary power of black churches in the African American community, their role is a serious piece of any discussion of African American religion and politics.

## Future Directions

The sections above lead us to our final question regarding the future of black theology. Black theology does have a future, yet it is one that must be immersed in the present and not built on romanticized notions of the black Christianity of the past. Black theologians cannot continue to cite the civil rights and black power movements as informing their current work. These have now become historical sources. Black theologians need to engage the Christianity of today and to entertain the fact that the study of Christianity gives one only a limited understanding of the complexity of African American religion. This final section explores the future of black theology in light of recent developments that point to new directions in the field. It concludes by addressing the question of redemptive suffering, a key issue within black theology that defines its past and future.

With the publication of J. Kameron Carter's *Race: A Theological Account*, a new challenged is raised, one to theologians of all races.[38] This groundbreaking monograph is the first of its kind to study race as a *theological* category. Fundamental to Carter's argument is the insistence that to truly understand race in contemporary intellectual discourse and society at large, a theological analysis of race is necessary. Similarly, Carter argues, one cannot understand racism without taking the centrality of religion into serious consideration. Carter takes an entirely new approach, arguing not only that race is a theological category but also that it has been since the first century. Theology, he argues, is part of the intellectual process of the construction of humanity as racialized. The basis of Carter's argument is the claim that, through their attempt to break from their Jewish foundation, early Christians created a racialized understanding of themselves that is now fundamental to modern constructions of race. Jews became the "other," and Western Christian identity was created in contrast to that other. Jews became associated with the East, and Christian identity became synonymous with the West. Western civilization became identical to Christianity. The West was deemed superior, and the groundwork was laid for a Christian understanding of white supremacy.

Carter begins by outlining the creation of this Western Christian, white-supremacist category of whiteness, and, in the later parts of his book, he offers a constructive reimagination of Christian identity. Carter argues that his selected texts lay the groundwork for an understanding of Jesus that does not allow him to be abstracted from his Jewish body. This abstraction of Jesus from his historical, physical body is a key moment in making Jesus white. Reconnecting Jesus to his Jewish body deconstructs the white supremacist notion of Christianity as synonymous with Western European culture. Carter situates the question of race as being at the heart of theology, not as a contemporary add-on by minority populations. His book forces all theologians to take race seriously and not to make it a "theme park," visited when discussing people of color exclusively. Carter also forces the question of the relevance of dominant, historical theology for black theology as a whole. Although in its early years black theology heavily emphasized the retrieval of African American theological sources as its primary starting point, today's black theologians are engaging traditional theology in a more intentional and systematic manner. I welcome this broadening of sources to include the Christian tradition as a whole, but I do worry that doing so will pull black theologians into the internalized debates of the limited intellectual conversation partners in contemporary theology.

Theologian Monica Coleman also expands the audience and task of theology through her serious engagement of the indigenous and African traditional strands within African American Christianity.[39] Although womanist theologians have acknowledged the non-Christian traditions in their scholarship, they always do so in the context of how they relate to Christianity. Womanists should examine the diversity that constitutes black religion and not limit the inclusion of non-Christian elements as appendices to a Christian center. If womanist theology is centered on the construction of black women's identity in light of religion, then womanist theologians must look at the totality of African American religion. Coleman acknowledges the impact of syncretized African traditional religions on African American Christianity. Her postmodern womanist theology, informed by process thought, emphasizes theological communities in which the individual cannot be saved outside of her community. Hers is a cosmological community that highlights the significance of the ancestors for African traditional religions. The ancestors represent one way in which the present experiences the past. For Coleman, when someone dies she becomes an ancestor. Ancestors commune together in the spiritual realm, which is another way of describing the nature of God. The ancestor becomes part of God's presence in the world. These ancestors are aligned with God's wishes for us. Coleman's work on ancestors has implications for how our notion of God is constructed, for the Holy Spirit can also be understood as an ancestor. Constructive, contextual, womanist theologies such as Coleman's push black theology into spaces that challenge its Christian center and that speak authentically about the opacity of black religion. She broadens the manner in which we think of Christian theological categories in light of non-Christian worldviews.

As the final two chapters of this book suggest, Coleman is not alone in making some first attempts to incorporate African traditional religious worldviews into black theology. However, such attempts are too few and far between. Black theology should recognize that its exclusive Christian worldview offers a limited and, frankly, false depiction of the complexity of African American religion in the United States. As Pinn reminds us, "This emphasis on 'non-Christian' orientation is a point of slow growth within Black theology because of a long-standing debate over the nature of theology, with most assuming it is by its very nature a theistic (and most properly Christian) enterprise."[40] This view is coupled with the assumption that Christianity is the dominant religious framework of African Americans. Black religion in the United States cannot be reduced to the Black Church or even to Christianity.

Perhaps at the root of this issue are absolutist Christian assertions that lead to a negative distancing from African religion and culture. Could it be that, through the acceptance of certain Christian claims, one is automatically absorbed into racist and cultural hierarchies? Theologian Jawanza Eric Clark argues, "The American racial hierarchy, which constructs the black person as the lowest racialized human being, is rooted in religious dogma and is derived from Christian construction of the African heathen. . . . Consequently, Black church theology has accepted a form of Christianity that belies and contradicts black people's African origins."[41] Clark sees this as an issue in particular for black Protestant Christians, whose churches were more theologically repressive than Catholicism. His scholarship emphasizes the development of a theological methodology grounded in African sources, which he believes is sympathetic ultimately to liberationist concerns. His work draws from the Akan worldview to offer an alternative anthropology that is not oppositional and dualistic and focuses on the ancestors. For Clark, the future of liberation theology is grounded in African traditional religious resources. Thus for black liberation theologians, the question of how non-Christian religions contribute to black liberation is key. Black liberation cannot be reduced to African American Christianity.

Too often black theologians describe the African American community as an exclusively oppressed people. The subject of African American religion cannot be limited to an oppressed object but instead should be a conveyer of cultural and religious meaning. This complex subjectivity is not limited to one dimension of identity or one religion; it presents African American religion as a site of agency and a space in which African Americans make meaning in their lives. This complex picture is radically different from the picture of African Americans one finds in most theologies, in which they are consistently defined exclusively as suffering and oppressed. This view is clearly expressed in the primacy of redemptive suffering within black theology.

Cone's most recent book raises the question of redemptive suffering in light of the cross and the practice of lynching African Americans. The cross and the lynching tree are both symbols of death, although one represents hope and the other white supremacy. And yet in the contemporary United States the cross has lost its prophetic power: "The cross has been transformed into a harmless, non-offensive ornament that Christians wear around their necks. Rather than reminding us of the 'cost of discipleship,' it has become a form of 'cheap grace,' an easy way to salvation that doesn't force us to confront the power of Christ's message and mission."[42] For Cone, the connection between the cross and the lynching tree must be made in order to save Christian America from the sins of slavery and white supremacy. The lynching tree reveals the meaning of the cross as a concrete image of human suffering; the cross does not allow the lynching tree to symbolize solely horrific suffering. Drawing from the imagery of Latin American liberation theologians, the cross places God in the midst of crucified peoples. Black religion is defined by suffering; it emerges from the suffering of African Americans struggling to make sense of their lives. The lynching tree reminds us of the historical suffering of African Americans and the scandal of the cross. In black theology this imagery is intimately linked to its understanding of the human as it is connected to Jesus's suffering on the cross.

A theological anthropology that privileges suffering bodies reveals the suffering body that is at the heart of Christianity. M. Shawn Copeland outlines five convictions that ground her theological anthropology: an understanding of the body as mediator of divine revelation; the significance of the body for shaping human existence as relational and social; an emphasis on the creativity of the triune God as revealed through differences in identity; an embodied understanding of solidarity; and the role of the Eucharist in ordering and transforming bodies. As she writes so provocatively, "The body provokes theology."[43] Basing her anthropological reflections on suffering black women's bodies, Copeland argues that slavery poses the greatest challenge to theological anthropology. Hers is a Eucharistic meditation on the body, for both the Eucharist and racism imply bodies. The Eucharist embodies Jesus's sacrificial gift of his life in order to bring his Father's mercy and love. Eucharistic solidarity is a countersign to violence to bodies; we are Jesus's body, and this calls for an embodied praxis of discipleship.

Copeland's emphasis on the body is an important one for all liberation theologies, especially as she recasts it through a sacramental lens. Liberation theologies constantly remind us of the reduction of marginalized peoples to their bodies, whether it is skin color, hair texture, or genitalia. In addition, the abuse of peoples bodies through human trafficking, forced labor, poorly paid labor, and torture are pressing theological issues in this contemporary globalized world. Copeland reminds Christian theologians that the importance of the body, however, goes well beyond social and political issues. The Eucharist (for Roman Catholics in particular) and the incarnation force us to infuse the body with theological value. Just as Carter emphasizes that race is a theological, not just a sociological, category, Copeland recasts embodiment as a theological question that forces us to delve deeply into the nature of the sacred and of human embodiment.

A theological emphasis on embodiment can lead to studies of dress and ornamentation in African American religion. Pinn points out that celebratory dress is used by African Americans in religious settings in response to the manner in which slaves were paraded on the auction block barely dressed: "This use of expressive or material culture was vital in that for enslaved blacks dress [it] has both visual and symbolic value, drawing attention to both their individuality and participation in community."[44] Clothing becomes a signifier of one's value in one's community and before God, in contrast to one's value as someone else's property. These sentiments are echoed in Butler's study of the intersection of dress and respectability for women in the Church of God in Christ. Respectable dress, as well as respect for the body through cleanliness and consumption, become a counterpoint to white racist assumptions about black bodies.[45] Both Butler and Pinn expand the study of black bodies beyond a reductionist emphasis on suffering to material culture and dress.

The debate over redemptive suffering and its meaning has saturated black theology; it is discussed not only by the theologians cited above but also by Delores Williams, Jones, and Pinn.[46] The meaning of suffering is a perennial Christian question that takes on special significance in light of the narrow definition in the United States of the African American community exclusively as a suffering people. Pinn argues that suffering does not have redemptive qualities and seeing it as such eclipses liberation activity.[47] This view fits neatly into the overall narrative of Christianity within black theology, one of a God that sides with and suffers with the oppressed. Yet such a narrow construction of African American identity erases the complexity of the African American community. In addition, the ambiguous equivalency of black and African American among the majority of black theologians obliterates the cultural complexity of the black community in the United States.

In the future black liberation theology needs to be more grounded than it is in the present. Black liberation theologians should be honest about their relationship with other scholars of religion, the academy as a whole, the church, and the broader public. They should stop clinging to a romanticized version of the Christianity of the past and, instead, critically examine the Christianity of the present. In addition, they cannot stop with Christianity. Black religion broadly conceived and African American religion narrowly conceived participate in a religious pluralism that is absent in the pages of black and womanist theologians. Although some scholars are making inroads in this direction, more work on the opacity and intricacy of black religion is needed. Black theology should come to terms with the cultural diversity of black peoples in the United States; they are not only African American, but also Caribbean and Latino/a.

3

# Latino/a Theology

*To Liberate or Not to Liberate?*

The inclusion of Latino/a theology in this book may be a point of contention, for whether Latino/a theologians describe themselves as liberation theologians, and therefore their collective body of work as liberationist, is a matter of debate. This is a fundamental question this chapter will explore, for it raises the broader issue of what defines theology as liberationist. Is it the self-proclamation by the author, or is it the theological and social commitments found in his or her work? Or is it the theological conversation partners that the author engages? These are core questions that challenge the very nature of liberation theology and how these scholars understand "allies" or coalitional partners.

Historical overviews of Latino/a theology have been published in various places, and this chapter is not meant to provide a detailed historical account of the events, culture, and organizations that informed the development of this theology. Instead, this chapter will situate Latino/a theology within the broader U.S. academic climate, in particular relating it to those themes, scholars, and developments that shape its discourse. Latino/a theology emerged initially from a strong Roman Catholic ethos, and the theological climate of a post-Vatican II U.S. Church and academy played a significant role in its development. This history distinguishes the work of Latino/a scholars significantly from the scholarship of black theologians, who emerged initially from a strong Protestant context rooted in historical black churches. Overviews of Latino/a theology highlight the significance of the *Encuentro* movement (a Roman Catholic pastoral plan for ministry among Latino/as) and the establishment of *los Padres* and *las Hermanas* (Latino/a organizations of priests and women religious) for nurturing the Roman Catholic pastoral setting of Latino/a theology. On the academic front, the explosion of Latin American liberation theology and racial/ethnic-minority theologies in the United States also plays a significant role in nurturing and challenging Latino/a theological voices.

The academic institutionalization of Latino/a theology began in the 1980s with the creation of the journal *Apuntes* and the formation of the Academy of Catholic Hispanic Theologians in the United States (ACH-TUS). During the early 1990s ACHTUS began publishing the *Journal of Hispanic/Latino Theology*. The establishment of journals and professional organizations dedicated to Latino/a theology cemented the academic presence of this theological discourse. Given the heavy Roman Catholic influence on early Latino/a theology, the Roman Catholic theological academy in the United States has been a significant conversation partner for Latino/a theologians.

This chapter focuses on several questions regarding the nature of, scope of, and audience for Latino/a theology. Although Latino/a theologians display significant diversity in their approaches, they nonetheless write about the existence of a collective Latino/a theology based on their shared emphasis on the Christian religious experiences of Latino/a peoples in the United States. Similarly, this understanding is based on a sense of shared scholarship. Latino/a theologians have a shared sense of collective identity, but the role of liberation theology in their writings is contested.

## Is Latino/a Theology a Liberation Theology?

The question of whether Latino/a theology is a liberation theology is a difficult one, for there is no consensus among the authors of this theology that their theological projects are liberationist. Often Latino/a theologians are grouped with other liberation theologians, given the use of the category of liberationist in Third World and U.S. minority theologies. In a similar vein, the prominence of certain Latina theologians who explicitly embrace a liberationist feminist framework adds to the complexity of the question. Rather than a social-justice issue such as racism, sexism, or economic injustice, it is often the category of culture that has united Latino/a theologians: "The defining role of culture and the critique of cultural oppression and of universalizing claims are themes that underlie most of Latino/a theology. The preferential option for culture, if we may be allowed the expression, characterizes Latino/a theology."[1] Although an emphasis on culture does not preclude an emphasis on social justice, it is nonetheless a point of departure from the more justice-centered work of liberation theologies. Often, as we saw in black liberation theology, an emphasis on culture is contrasted to an emphasis on social justice.

Latino/a theologians themselves are undecided on the issue. If one, for example, takes as a case study the work of Latina theologians, one sees that the use of a feminist, and therefore liberationist, hermeneutic is a site of contention. Latina feminist theologians are those scholars who situate themselves within the broader networks of liberation theologies and feminist theologies globally. Latina feminist theologians privilege Latina experiences of poverty and oppression. This emphasis on marginalization is also found in the work of Latina theologians who are not explicitly feminist. Latina theologian Ana María Pineda, for example, does not categorize her scholarship as explicitly feminist. Pineda can be categorized in a pastoral theologian. In spite of the groundbreaking contributions of Ada María Isasi-Díaz and María Pilar Aquino, the most recognized Latina theologians, who quite explicitly understand their work as feminist and liberationist, not all Latina theologians are feminist. Unlike their feminist colleagues, pastorally focused Latina theologians emphasize ministry within the Latino/a community.[2] These pastoral Latina theologians do not outright reject the label of feminist or liberationist, yet they also clearly do not self-identify as liberation theologians. Similarly, much of their scholarship does not reflect a systematic engagement with liberation theologies.

There exists a third group of Latina theologians, Protestant and evangelical Latinas. This group of Latina theologians rejects any sort of feminist hermeneutic. Loida Martell-Ortero, in her theology of *mujeres evangélicas,* expresses reservations about both Latina feminist and *mujerista* theologies because of their Roman Catholic emphasis and what she sees as their secular origins.[3] Martell-Ortero articulates, as an alternative, her theology *evangélica,* whose sources are found in the faith and practices of Protestant Latina women. She is critical of the blind categorization of all Latina voices as "feminist." What is unclear in the writings of these second two groups of Latina scholars is whether their implicit or direct rejection of the feminist label implies a rejection of their theologies as liberationist.

In addition to debates surrounding whether one is liberationist, the frequent categorization of Latino/a theology as a contextual theology, in contrast to a liberation theology, adds another element to the discussion. Definitions of Latino/a theology as contextual theology abound: "To the extent that Latino/a theology proceeds from an acknowledgement and affirmation of its particular context in history, it is considered one of the many 'contextual theologies' presently being developed."[4] In their introduction to Latino/a theology, theologians Miguel De La Torre and Edwin Aponte list six functions of Latino/a theology: understanding the divine from within Latino/a culture; discerning God's liberative will in the face of oppression (both cultural and economic); proclaiming salvation and liberation for Latino/a culture in all its diversity; creating "theological harmony" between the bible and the Latino/a condition; challenging the dominant culture's misconceptions about Latino/as; and embodying a prophetic voice against the dominant white theology.[5] They later define Latino/a theology as "the Latino/a voice of faith."[6] It is clear that they understand Latino/a theology as a contextual theology that also contains liberative elements.

Numerous Latino/a theologians contend that Latino/a theology has been influenced by liberation theology and contains various methodological elements that characterize it as liberationist; these factors include a concern for oppressed communities, an emphasis on the contextual nature of theology, and an emphasis on the cultural production of marginalized peoples.[7] Liberationist methodological patterns in Latino/a theology include a critical reading of the contemporary context of Latino/as; the use of concrete voices of Latino/as in the theology; the use of autobiography and critical denunciation; and a utopian vision. Although there exist liberationist strands within some Latino/a theologians, Latino/a theology as a whole is not a self-proclaimed liberation theology. Does this mean that Latino/a theology offers a counterpoint to Latin American and other liberationist discourses? Far from it; however, although Latino/a theology that has always claimed to express the faith of the people, the faith of the people is not necessarily liberationist. Liberation ecclesiologies are present in only a small percentage of Latino/a churches. In fact, Christianity among Latino/as is becoming increasingly *evangélico*; it is characterized by a more conservative theology that does not emphasize the social-transformative action so fundamental to the work of liberation theologians. This characterization leads us to ask, What makes liberation theology liberationist: the subject matter of the scholarship or the author? Latino/a theologians have made a significant effort to present the Latino/a community as a marginalized and oppressed community in the United States. Does writing a theology on behalf of or about an oppressed community automatically make a theology liberationist?

There are plenty of scholars in the field of religion and theology who write about marginalized communities but who do not claim a liberationist voice. Fernando Segovia has framed this question as being about the Latino/a critic as individual and agent.[8] One can easily find, for example, black biblical scholars who never make a reference to their identity or to a broader sense of their ethnic or racial group in their research. Such persons could be described as biblical scholars who are black. But are they black biblical scholars? Similarly one can find a white Anglo scholar of religion who works closely with the Latino/a community, knows the language, and focuses his or her academic research on that community. For many, that person cannot be called a Latino/a theologian because he or she is not Latino/a. And yet, how would one categorize the work, which is informed by and gives voice to the Latino/a community? Another way of framing this question is to ask what makes Latino/a theology Latino/a. The box that the author checks on his or her government census form or the community that informs his or her work? When Segovia defines Latino/a American biblical criticism and pedagogy as a combination of membership and conscientization, he is focusing on the author. This begs the question for Segovia, and for Latino/a theologians as a whole, if anything about the subject or focus of one's research becomes reflective of its minority status. In other words, is the emphasis on the author or the content?

To reframe the questioned liberationist status of Latino/a theology, one should therefore ask whether focusing on a marginalized community in the United States, such as Latino/as, is what makes Latino/a theology liberationist. The answer is no, as can be clearly seen in the work of pastoral and evangelical Latina theologians who emphasize marginalization within the Latino/a community but are not liberation theologians. The hermeneutical and methodological framework of the author determines this categorization. Therefore, it is impossible to say that all Latino/a theology is liberationist. Some Latino/a theologians explicitly embrace a liberationist framework and are self-proclaimed liberation theologians. However, others either reject or do not explicitly engage such a categorization of their scholarship.

## Latino/a Theology's Public

Linked to the question of the liberationist nature of Latino/a theology is the question of audience and intention. Latino/a theology addresses primarily two publics: the ecclesial realm and, increasingly, the North American theological academy. Unless Latino/a theologians broaden the intended audiences and interlocutors of their scholarship, their theological work will have little impact outside these realms. The implicit assumption that theology is only for and in the Church greatly limits Latino/a theology's public. Latino/a theology has historically been closely tied to ecclesial concerns.[9] While this emphasis is not problematic, the reduction of Latino/a theology to the ecclesial realm limits the scope of this theology. Many of the Latino/as whom Latino/a theologians claim to represent understand their spirituality in much broader terms.

The roots of Latino/a theology are clearly pastoral, embodied perhaps most concretely in its founding father, Virgilio Elizondo. Elizondo's scholarship is thoroughly grounded in his grassroots ministry through the Mexican American Cultural Center, which he founded in 1972, and his service as rector of the San Fernando Cathedral in San Antonio, Texas, from 1983 to 1995. He is, at his core, a pastoral theologian and minister. It is not surprising that the book published in his honor begins with a section on "Religious Education as Pastoral Theology."[10] A key thrust of the pastoral dimension of Elizondo's theology is his commitment to making the faith and the everyday struggles of the Mexican American people a starting point of his theology. Theology cannot be written in isolation, and it cannot be elaborated by exterior sources. Instead, theology must always remain rooted in and engaged with the community from which it emerges. Elizondo writes, "Theology cannot be imported. Neither can it be developed in isolation from the believing and practicing community. It is a joint enterprise of a believing community, which is seeking the meaning of its faith and the direction of its journey of hope lived in the context of charity."[11] Methodologically, Elizondo's understanding of the communal dimension of theology refutes the notion of the theologian as an isolated individual working on abstract material. Instead, the theologian is engaged with the concrete faith and life of the people in a pastoral setting. The people shape Elizondo's theology; he does not attempt to fit his theological conceptions into abstract, preconceived notions of theological loci.

The primary academic public of Latino/a theology is the Euro-American theological academy. Because this is the dominant discourse, this audience can limit Latino/a theology's agenda, for Euro-American theology's concerns are often not connected to or reflective of its communities of accountability. Often efforts are made to take traditional theology and flavor it with Latino/a culture and religion. The 1999 volume in Latino/a Catholic systematic theology entitled *From the Heart of Our People* begins with the question, "What would Catholic systematics look like if it were done *latinamente?*"[12] Glancing at the table of contents of this book, however, one wonders whether its success can be measured by its connection, or lack thereof, to Latino/a faith communities. Sure, there are articles with the words *tierra, pueblo, fiesta,* and *convivencia,* in the titles. Yet, these Spanish words mask traditional Roman Catholic systematic theology. Although this book was an attempt to do Latino/a Catholic systematic theology, what it reflects is a European-born systematic theology flavored with the spices of Latino/a culture. The language has changed, but the theological positions covered in the book remain within the normative paradigm.[13]

The academic context of Latino/a theology is becoming increasingly prominent. This academic emphasis has become stronger throughout the development of Latino/a theology, in spite of continued attention to the pastoral project. Theologian Harold Recinos suggests that "Latino/a theology has been steadily building a contextual liberation theology in the United States that encompasses the varieties of religious experiences found within Latino/a communities. The early stages of Latino/a theological production were more closely tied to grassroots communities and practical pastoral concerns, while more recent work is intentionally seeking to find a voice in the academy and in public theology."[14] This is a significant development that is directly connected to Latino/a theology's methodology. If Latino/a theology in its early phases began as a theological voice that was rooted in grassroots pastoral communities and concerns, and if today it is more academic in its focus, then where is contemporary Latino/a theology based?

Latino/a theologians also operate with a privileging of the Christian religion that marginalizes non-Christian religions within Latino/a religious life. Although there is a growing emphasis on the non-Christian elements of Latino/a religious worldviews and practices, it is always approached through a Christian framework. Yet Latino/a scholars often use with ease the cultural and religious production of indigenous and African peoples as sources for theological reflection while simultaneously maintaining a dominant Christian paradigm within the construction of Latino/a identity and religiosity. They do this without acknowledging the function of power within their academic appropriation of non-Christian and non-European sources. This lack of acknowledgment is seen most sharply in the Christian starting point of Latino/a theologies and the ways in which non-Christian sources and cultures are misused in Latino/a discourse.

Latino/a theologians approach Latino/a religion from a Christian foundation, adding the flavors of African and indigenous America as they see fit. A much welcome alternative to this paradigm is historian Edwin Aponte's work on *botánicas* (small stores that sell religious articles and supplies; in them practitioners of a variety of religious faiths often offer spiritual consultations and faith healings). As noted by Aponte, the *botánica* has become "a place of wider spiritual significance and increasingly eclectic metaphysical blending. But metaphysical blending does not necessarily mean that the distinctions between religious traditions are forgotten or obliterated."[15] Latino/a Christians who self-identify as Christian readily enter into spaces such as *botánicas* as part of their everyday religious lives.[16] The pluralism evident in *botánicas* is complex and crosses the boundaries of official religions. Aponte concludes that Latino/a spirituality is overwhelmingly a Spanglish spirituality, one that is a hybrid, sometimes messy, and that at times blurs the borders that separate institutionalized religions. Aponte encourages Latino/a scholars to develop research tools to address Latino/a religious "boundary crossings," a suggestion that resonates strongly with the spirit of this book.

## The Subjects of Latino/a Theology

The question of identity is central to Latino/a theology. These reflections on Latino/a identity fall broadly into two categories: attempting to define what is Latino/a about Latino/a theological discourse and offering an authentic, thick description of the Latino/a community in all its diversity in the United States. Latino/a theology has been marked by the contention that there is an authenticity to its theological claims about Latino/as *as* Latino/as. Yet, how one identifies with and participates in Latino/a culture and communities varies from community to community. Similarly, many non-Latino/a theological scholars have substantial commitments to Latino/a communities, yet these scholars are often sidelined as inauthentic. In overemphasizing their "theological birthright," Latino/a theologians have created a dangerous and limited understanding of their theological contributions. First, they have created an "us" and "them" regarding who has an "authentic" theological voice. Second, and more important for their broader contributions to the theological public, the claim that a Latino/a has the most authentic voice about Latino/as automatically leads to the claim that their writings on non-Latino/a topics are not as authentic. This claim limits their work to Latino/a communities, thus eclipsing their theological scholarship in the broader field, which remains dominated by European and Euro-American thinkers. There is something unsettling about an academic discourse being reduced to the author's birthplace, heritage, and/or native language.

If one claims that a non-Latino/a cannot write Latino/a theology, then the relationship to non-Latino/as who write about Latino/as becomes problematic: If the task of Latino/a theology is defined as giving voice to poor Latino/as, does one have to be Latino/a to do Latino/a theology?[17] Latino/a theologians claim a authenticity for their academic research based on their nation of origin (or their parents' or even grandparents' nation of origin). But if Latino/a theology is truly attempting to have the academy become its primary public, such claims will not be well received. Indeed, it is fascinating to speculate about why such debates do not frame scholarship on religion from a nontheological perspective. Perhaps the reason is that Latino/a theologians are aware that their minority status can open avenues within the theological academy. Latino/a Catholic theologians, in particular, can use this claim to make a persuasive case for their increased representation based on the growing Latino/a face of Catholicism in the United States. Yet this case for relevancy based on demographics is dangerous. Such rhetoric automatically renders minority Catholic populations, African American and Asian American, irrelevant because of their small numbers.

The broad categorization of all Latino/as as poor and oppressed is a caricature of the community, similar to the "ontological blackness" Victor Anderson highlights in black theology. Latino/a theology needs to address those Latino/as who have achieved a certain level of political, economic, and social success in the United States. Not all Latino/as are poor, and not all self-identify as oppressed. Many Latino/as are successful. Geography also plays a significant role in the U.S. Latino/a experience. The following statement does not ring true for all Latino/as: "Most Hispanics continue to be seen by the dominant culture as exiles, aliens, and outsiders, regardless of their historical connection to U.S. lands. To be Latino/a within the United States is never to belong, unless the person can 'pass' for a Euroamerican."[18] The complexity of the Latino/a community needs to be examined within Latino/a theologies.

One could respond that marginalized and poor Latino/as are the sole emphasis of Latino/a theology. In other words, Latino/a theologians are not writing for and about all Latino/as, they are writing exclusively for poor and oppressed Latino/as. Yet Latino/a theologians can be seen as part of an elite—given their educational backgrounds—and middle class—given their positions in North American universities. Although one could argue that they are marginalized within the theological academy, they are not in any way disenfranchised in the same ways as the poor, oppressed Latino/as they claim to represent. In order to be accountable to these communities, the foundation of their work should be a concrete connection to the faith life of poor and oppressed Latino/as.

Race, class, gender, sexual orientation, immigration status, and generation are some of the markers of the diversity within Latino/a communities. Younger generations need to be more explicit sources for Latino/a theology. Often Latino/a theologians frame the construction of Latino/a

identity as diametrically opposed to the dominant construction of identity in the United States. The rejection of the U.S. element leaves young
Latino/as denying a significant portion of their identity. "Second- and
third- generation Latino/as," theologian Michael Lee writes, "exhibit a
biculturalism that is not quite captured in the work of earlier Latino/a
Christology and its challenge could help fashion the agenda of the next
generation."[19] Although these comments focus on the development of a
Latino/a Christology, they ring true for Latino/a theology as a whole. Second and third generation Latino/as, especially those born in the United
States, find little of their culture and experience reflected in the pages of
Latino/a theology, which often privileges the voices of the *abuelitas*, or
elders, at the expense of youth. Linked to this discrepancy is Latino/a
theology's use of the terms *the people* and *popular* without defining them
clearly.[20] Another layer of complexity is the growing Protestant population among Latino/as and the manner in which their religious life shapes
Latino/a theology. Latino/a *evangélicos* have been largely absent from
U.S. religious history.[21] They have also been marginalized within Latino/a
theology. This situation is slowly changing, although the Roman Catholic
ethos from which Latino/a theology emerged continues to dominate its
agenda.[22]

## Latino/a Theology's Method

The fundamental starting point of Latino/a theology is the lived religious
practices of Latino/a Christian communities throughout the United
States. The emphasis is overwhelmingly ecclesial, while nodding to the
fact that many Latino/a religious practices exist on the border of Christian ecclesial structures and, in some cases, incorporate non-Christian
elements within them. Latino/a theologians struggle to negotiate their
strong commitment to Latino/a theological categories that speak to the
lived reality of Latino/a faith while simultaneously remaining equally
committed to the traditional categories of theological discourse that have
been classically articulated throughout the centuries.

Broad definitions of Latino/a theology exist, such as: "Latino/a theology has taken up the task of reflecting on the articulated faith and religious symbols and practices of Hispanics in the United States in light of their cultural, economic, and social context/situation."[23] More particular definitions focus on distinctive denominations: "Latino/a Pentecostal theology is rooted in an experiential, oral, and lived tradition. Theology that is sung, felt, and experienced through the person of the Holy Spirit."[24] These two definitions, as well as the other definitions explored previously in this chapter, share an emphasis on the Latino/a and theological. We have already discussed Latino/a identity. This section explores the privileging of theology among Latino/a theologians as the exclusive discipline to describe and account for Latino/a faith life. Latino/a theologians should become more interdisciplinary in their scholarship. Their heavy theological legacy has cut off Latino/a voices from broader analyses of Latino/a religion. This section will use Latino/a theology's privileging of popular religion as a case study to demonstrate the need for more interdisciplinary work.

Latino/a theology's emphasis on the theological academy as the primary, and often exclusive, conversation partner limits its scope. It is curious that Latino/a theologians do not enter into dialogue with area studies, ethnic studies, critical race theory, and the social sciences in a more explicit manner to enrich their discussions of Latino/a identity and faith life. It is also a concern that within Latino/a Studies, an interdisciplinary venture, Latino/a theology is not a conversation partner. It would seem an obvious entry point for Latino/a theologians who write about the concrete faith life of Latino/as and who desire to have the academy as their primary locus. In addition, such broadening of Latino/a theology's method would enhance understandings of the complexity of Latino/a religion in ecclesial, civic, and public life.

In spite of the heavy theological emphasis of Latino/a scholarship on religion, new voices are slowly beginning to emerge that argue for a broader interdisciplinary perspective and a more explicit engagement of disciplines outside theology. Noting the groundbreaking work

of scholars such as Elizondo, Gastón Espinosa emphasizes anthropologist David Carrasco's corpus (based on a religious studies approach that
examined indigenous religions) as a methodological "break" with the
theological orientation of the study of Latino/a religion, although not
an ideological one.[25] In his own research Espinosa proposes a "*Nepantla*-
based ethnophenomenological method as one of many possible alterna-
tives to rethink how one goes about studying and interpreting Mexican-American religions at secular colleges and universities where one is
required not to promote or endorse a theological worldview."[26] Evoking
the Nahuatl words for "land in the middle," Espinosa hopes to narrow
the gap between religious studies and theology through an interdisciplinary approach that attempts to respect both the insider and the outsider
within the religious traditions. Espinosa's rejection of the false dichotomy
between theology and religious studies is commendable, but even more
important is his problematization of the insider/outsider role in the
scholarship. His interdisciplinary and multidisciplinary approach does
not preclude advocacy for marginalized communities. Latino/a theologians have yet to substantially address this question because they are all
assumed insiders of the discourse they have constructed. However, some
are more inside than others, and many are on the outside.

Espinosa is not alone. His co-edited volume (with Virgilio Elizondo
and Jesse Miranda) on Latino/a religious civic activism demonstrates
not only a methodological broadening of the study of Latino/a religion
but also an expansion of the project to examine Latino/a faith-based
political activism within public life.[27] Other publications accompany this
methodological shift, including Luis D. León's research on religion in
the borderlands between the United States and Mexico. León not only
wants to study religion on the geographic borderlands but also between
the boundaries created by scholars of religion who are describing lived
religious practices. For León, the religious practices of Mexican Americans function in part as a way of confronting crises in everyday life. These
religious practices occur in the borderlands and are at times in direct
conflict with institutional religion.[28]

In addition to scholars such as Espinosa and León who are calling for a broadening of Latino/a theology's methodology, a group of social historians are approaching Latino/a religious life through historical and anthropological methodologies that can both inform and challenge Latino/a theology's approach. Historian David Badillo examines Latino/a Catholicism through a historical study of urbanism in various U.S. cities. His comprehensive work looks not only at institutional Catholicism but also at lived Catholicism, and his emphasis on particular Latino/a communities challenges broad, overarching assumptions about Latino/a Catholics as a whole.[29] Historian Timothy Matovina has done extensive work on Latino/a religious history, particularly among Mexican American Catholics, that is based on solid historical and ethnographic research. This work is perhaps best exemplified in his study on devotion to Our Lady of Guadalupe at the San Fernando Cathedral in San Antonio, Texas. Matovina traces the history of this devotion and ends with a description of the contemporary lived religion surrounding her. He tells the story of the Mexican-American community in San Antonio through her story, interweaving narratives of race, urban development, and religion.[30] Adding to the chorus of historians, Thomas Tweed's ethnographic study of Cuban American devotion to Our Lady of Charity also offers a much-needed, ground-level approach to the concrete faith communities surrounding this extremely popular and visible Marian devotion among Cubans in the Miami diaspora.[31]

In a similar methodological vein Kristy Nabhan-Warren's book, *The Virgin of El Barrio: Marian Apparitions, Catholic Evangelizing, and Mexican American Activism*, highlights a Mexican American Marian devotion that both participates in and exists outside of institutional Catholicism. Combining history and ethnography, Nabhan-Warren's book studies the religious life surrounding the backyard shrine belonging to Estela Ruiz, a woman who began to have visions of the Virgin Mary in South Phoenix and from whom has emerged a Catholic evangelizing group (Mary's Ministries) and a social-justice sister group (ESPIRITU). The book traces the history of the messages from Mary and the emergent communities. More important for this study, "Estela, her family, and the many pilgrims who come to the shrine and involve themselves in Mary's Ministries and ESPIRITU have stories to tell that can shed light on how we understand the construction and overlap of American Catholic, Mexican American, evangelical, class, and gendered identities, and how those understandings might be revised according to a changing cultural landscape."[32] Nabhan-Warren argues that the shrine creates an alternative Catholic space that demonstrates a lived Catholicism that is the future of Latino/a Catholicism, in spite of the fact that the shrine devotees are all adherents to institutional Catholicism. Members of the Mary's Ministries are all extremely charismatic and *evangélico* in their spirituality and understanding of evangelization. They believe in faith healing, glossolalia (speaking in tongues, possession by the Holy Spirit), and a public expression of evangelization in order to counter growing Pentecostalism in their communities.

Similarly, numerous scholars of Latino/a religion have been publishing socioscientific research on Latino/a religion broadly. The Program for the Analysis of Religion among Latinos published numerous books on Latino/a religion from a wide variety of socioscientific perspectives in the mid-1990s.[33] Socioscientists such as Otto Maduro, Milagros Peña, Anthony M. Stevens-Arroyo, Gilbert Cadena, Gastón Espinosa, and Ana María Díaz-Stevens have made a significant contribution to the study of Latino/a religion in dialogue with Latino/a theologians. However, as Espinosa laments, "the future of Latino social science research on religion looks bleak."[34] There is a need for more scholars and the development of new methodologies.

Latino/a theology's privileging of the category of popular religion provides an example of how Latino/a theologians have limited their broader academic conversations. Contrary to Latin American liberation theologians, Latino/a theologians add the element of justice, power, and marginalization into their definition of Latino/a theology, at times defining it as a form of liberation theology.[35] Popular religion becomes a means for the marginalized to express their religious faith. In sharp contrast to

Latin American liberation theology, within Latino/a theology, one does not find debates about whether popular religion is liberating. Latino/a theologians often define popular religion as the religion of an oppressed or marginalized community and as being linked to liberation. Popular religion, frequently, is presented as that which is most authentically Latino/a.[36] "The religion is 'popular' because the disenfranchised are responsible for its creation, making it a religion of the marginalized."[37] Yet not all definitions of popular religion consider it exclusively the religion of the oppressed. Some emphasize inculturation or context in contrast to liberation. These definitions imply that any group can express its religious faith through popular religion.

Perhaps no other scholar has written more on popular religion than Cuban American theologian Orlando O. Espín, who argues, "Popular religion seems to be an omnipresent phenomenon among U.S. Latinos."[38] Popular religion is related to normative religion, yet, in contrast to the official religion of the "experts," it involves a rereading and reemphasis of tradition Popular Catholicism, it is defined as a rereading of official Catholicism and as producing a "people's own version of the religion."[39] In later work, Espín emphasizes the epistemic value of popular Christianity as bearer of the Christian tradition. "Popular Christianity acts as an indispensable lens through which revelation, as received and elaborated by the *sensus fidelium* within Christianity, evolves and adapts itself to ordinary Christians' ever-changing sociocultural and historical circumstances."[40] Although Espín's claims are sound, the jump that is often made to stating that popular religion is somehow a privileged space for Latino/as is not accurate: popular religion appears in every religious tradition among every ethnic and racial group.

Popular Catholicism expresses a critical realism that cannot be reduced to the Latino/a community. Latino/a popular Catholicism is defined as the rituals that express Latino/a faith. Yet is this not the case for all Catholics? Often Latino/a theologians highlight Mexican American popular practices—like *posadas, Via Crucis,* and the Day of the Dead—as demonstrating that the way of being for Latino/a Catholics is centered on relationships (familial, communal, and cosmic) and that "the Catholicism of Latinos and Latinas, therefore, tends to be a Catholicism rooted, first [of all], not in the parish but in the home, in the neighborhood."[41] Is this not true for immigrant Catholicism as a whole? Although we can acknowledge the distinctiveness of Latino/a Catholics in relation to immigration, the influence of indigenous and African religions, and the colonial legacy of the Spanish church, it is not clear that Latino/as are that different from other immigrant Catholics in regard to the popular Catholicism within their communities.

The centrality of popular Catholicism or popular religion within Latino/a theology is unquestionable. Linked to the foundational writings of Elizondo, this theme, in particular, has been discussed by numerous Latino/a theologians in multiple contexts. Espín argues that it is impossible to write Latino/a theology without writing about Elizondo's foundational claims about popular Catholicism, which in Espín's eyes established the field of popular Catholicism within theology. The role of theology, he states, is to serve Christian communities, not to glorify the theologian. Espín presents Elizondo not only as initiating the theological study of popular Catholicism, but, in an echo of our previous discussion of Latino/a theology's public, as establishing the pastoral impulse behind this methodological shift, thus positioning the theological task within pastoral theology.[42]

Elizondo connects the centrality of popular religion to the emphasis on culture and identity found throughout the writings of Latino/a theologians, emphasizing that these practices exist at times on the border of institutional Catholicism. Elizondo argues that these rituals represent the core identity of a community and that they have an ambiguous relationship with the institutional church.[43] Although Elizondo's work is foundational for understanding popular religion among Latino/as, he is not the first or only scholar to examine popular Catholicism as central to understanding Catholic life in the United States. Similarly, the view that popular religion is the quintessential contribution to contemporary theology implies an inherent and exclusive *latinidad* to popular religion that is untrue. Latino/a theologians have continued to write about Latino/a popular religion or popular Catholicism, paying little attention to academic discussions surrounding the problematic nature of this category.

A critical assessment of the term *popular religion* is found in the work of Robert Orsi, who highlights the manner in which the term is problematic within academic discourse. Orsi argues that the designator *popular* automatically creates the normative character of religion that is unqualified.[44] The term *popular* marginalizes practices categorized as such in the academic study of religion and renders popular practices secondary in institutional ecclesial history.[45] Orsi also notes that the term was often associated with devotionals and rituals in the United States. As a resolution of this problem, he offers the term *lived religion*, a category that "directs attention to institutions *and* persons, texts *and* rituals, practices *and* theology, things *and* ideas—all as media of making and unmaking worlds."[46] Lived religion examines concrete historical communities within a broad social, historical, and institutional framework. Scholars of immigrant Catholicism such as Orsi challenge the assumption that Latino/as introduced the category of popular religion into the discipline and also challenge Latino/a theologians' use of the term.

Discussion surrounding the use of the term *popular religion* is also occurring within the context of the study of Latino/a lived religion. Historian and ethnographer Meredith McGuire highlights many of the concerns raised by Orsi in her work on Latino/a lived religion. Embracing the category *lived religion* because of the ambiguity in the term *popular religion*, McGuire argues that popular religion is contained in the term *lived religion*. While *popular religion* implies nonofficial religion, *lived religion* embraces popular religion within the web of everyday and institutional life.[47] *Lived religion* includes popular religion and official religion and does not allow the historic denigration of popular religion as irrelevant and often ignorant superstition.

Latino/a theologians' elaborations on popular religion emphasize its contextual nature, its location in everyday life, and the function of power, perhaps most clearly seen in the ambiguous and porous relationship between the institutional and popular church. Popular religion is "popular" as opposed to "orthodox" because of its marginalization by orthodoxy. The impulse behind Latino/a popular religion is not to stand in contrast to or to critique orthodoxy. However, in some instances the social location of Latino/as has forced Latino/a religious practices to be marginalized. In its primary form, popular religion is not intended in any way to be subversive, yet in refusing to be silenced, rejected, and ignored, it becomes so. However, popular religion always needs to be understood in light of broader institutional and social religion. The risk is that studies of popular religion can become reduced to personal devotions: "The danger of this approach is that, in its effort to document local everyday religious practices, it may lose sight of the institutional, structural, and systematic processes in which these practices are embedded; the decontextualization of popular religion may in turn lead to a failure to recognize the multiple ways in which power and resistance shape and are shaped by religion."[48] There needs to be a balance between the study of lived, local religion and its role in broader religious movements and institutional histories.

In spite of this groundbreaking scholarship on popular religion, much more needs to be done, especially in the area of theology. Scholars such as Espín have done vital work in exploring the theological function of popular religion and demonstrating how it is a bearer of tradition. Espín and others have begun some initial research on these religious practices as liberative for Latino/a communities. This is one piece of the picture. Although popular religious practices such as the *Via Crucis* have a political function because of, among other things, their highly public role and the prominence of the Latino/a community within them, the theology behind these rituals is not necessarily consonant with liberationist, political commitments. To put it bluntly, some popular religious practices are in contrast to the impulses of liberation theologies.

Latino/a theologians often define popular religion as religiosity that has been excluded by the dominant, institutionalized Church. This exclusion can range from a mild categorization of a practice as a cultural or ethnic expression to the more extreme rejection of a practice as un-Christian. Some religious practices are "tolerated" by the institutional Church because a certain ethnic group deems them important; churches that want to disassociate themselves from that particular practice or devotion blatantly condemn others. However, the tension between popular and institutional practices does not mean that popular and institutional religions are antithetical. In fact, many popular religious practices are situated within the confines of the institutional Church. This situation opens up a broader discussion of the relationship between religious practices labeled "popular" and the manner in which they are distinguished from institutional ones. Although, for many scholars of religion, popular religion is defined as the practices of the people in contrast to the practices of the elite, this perspective denies that the elite practice popular religion. Popular religion is linked to official religion, and one can never completely divorce the two. Engaging in an interdisciplinary debate surrounding the viability of popular religion and popular Catholicism would be a fruitful dialogue for Latino/a theologians.

## Future Directions

Latino/a theologians make a significant contribution to the study of Latino/a faith life through the discipline of theology. Although this contribution is critical, the goal of this chapter is to move this theology forward as it continues to develop and thrive. Nabhan-Warren's book on the backyard shrine and its emergent ministries is the result of ten years of ethnographic research—ten years of visiting the shrine, conducting countless interviews, and studying the history surrounding the community to be able to offer a complex "thick description" of the lived Catholicism of this community. Only then did she move to make some broad theological claims about the meaning of this devotion. What is striking is the amount of time and research this research took and the ease and frequency with which some Latino/a theologians, sometimes claiming to speak for all Latino/as, write books about Latino/a religious life yet do not reflect any concrete and long-term engagement with specific Latino/a faith communities.

All Latino/a theologians do not need to research their books for a decade or to become ethnographers. Yet they should be explicit about the lived religious sources that inform their claims about Latino/a religious life as a whole or even about particular ethnic groups. Cuban American theologian Jorge Aquino raises a similar criticism in his assessment of Roberto Goizueta's theology: "While emphasizing that his option for the poor must be established on the relationships with living, flesh-and-blood people, *no poor person speaks for herself in this text*. Where Goizueta invokes supposedly living persons, they are neither named nor quoted directly. This has the effect of authorizing the author's positions on U.S. Hispanic popular Catholicism without letting his sources speak for themselves."[49] Aquino rightfully points out that Goizueta, like many other Latino/a theologians, claims to be the voice "of the people" yet does not give the people a voice. Notable exceptions are found in the work of Ada María Isasi-Díaz and Jeanette Rodríguez, both of whom use ethnography and interviews as part of their methodologies. If Latino/a theologians are going to continue to speak on behalf of "the people," they should establish what gives them the right and insight to do so. This task is especially pressing given the trend toward increased academic engagement rather than pastoral engagement.

Although not a monograph, the book *Horizons of the Sacred: Mexican Traditions in U.S. Catholicism* offers the type of concrete, grounded research that more Latino/a theologians need to embrace.[50] The book combines on-the-ground research in history, ethnography, anthropology, and religious studies on various Mexican American religious devotions. The last two chapters provide theological reflection on these distinctive religious practices. The theological claims in the book are grounded in these case studies, not in abstract reflection on Latino/a religious practices as a whole.

The use of the category *popular religion* is problematic within Latino/a theology, for its defenders do not adequately acknowledge the use of the

term in other fields of religious studies, and they do not engage in important debates about the viability of this term. In other words, Latino/a
theologians act as if they invented the category of popular religion for
theology as a whole, as if they are the first to take concrete religious life
as the starting point for the study of religion. It is clear that popular religion and everyday life are categories embraced by feminist theologians
and scholars of religion within other disciplines. It is also clear that the
category of popular religion is problematic. Speaking of the Ruiz shrine,
Nabhan-Warren argues, "The faith courses, with their blending of institutional and grassroots, backyard Catholicism, directly challenge the traditional dichotomies that scholars of Catholicism have set up between
official and popular piety, and between Catholicism and evangelicalism,
pointing to both overlap and contestation."[51] Her statement reemphasizes
the point that although one can speak of popular religion and claim it
is in no way in conflict with or antithetical to official religion, the dualism is implied in the term. Therefore, the use of the term *lived Catholicism* or *grassroots Catholicism* is a much more accurate way to describe
the Catholicism Latino/a theologians claim to be writing about in their
works.

The ambiguity in determining the role of liberation within Latino/a
theology is a significant challenge to how liberation theology has been
traditionally understood. In other words, the indeterminate status of
Latino/a theology presents us with an exciting moment to redefine liberation theology, forcing it out of its traditionally narrow confines. This
redefinition comes from both the emphasis on context in Latino/a theology and the work some Latino/a theologians are doing to broaden the
category of liberation. Contextualizing her work in light of the ideas of
the Pentecostal theologians Samuel Soliván and Edwin Villafañe, Arlene
Sánchez Walsh presents Pentecostalism not only as liberative within the
faith context but also as liberating in relation to structural oppression.
Sánchez Walsh however nuances how she understands liberation, noting that it does not automatically equal liberation theology: "Defining
'liberation' in overly political terms—in theological terms that privilege

Catholic teaching rather than evangelical belief—has not generally been a part of the Pentecostal overview of who Jesus is. . . . For some, however, appropriating 'liberation' without affixing 'theology' next to it tends to ruin categories that are invested with as much theological currency as political currency." Instead the emphasis is on Jesus as liberator/healer.[52] Liberation is not always seen through a political lens in Latino/a theology.

Goizueta's most recent work attempts to articulate a liberation theological aesthetics that does not polarize the aesthetic and the liberative.[53] Often, a hasty interpretation of aesthetics leads to an understanding of it as downplaying or obscuring the significance of ethics and social justice.[54] However, an emphasis on Beauty does not have to be at the expense of the Good and can in fact inform one's commitment to social justice.[55] These insights contribute to a recasting of liberation theology that takes seriously ritual, culture, and context. The ambiguity surrounding whether Latino/a theology is a liberation theology challenges future scholarship for Latino/as in particular and liberation theologians as a whole. In addition, the presence of African diaspora and indigenous religions among Latino/as challenges the exclusive Christian framework of Latino/a theology.

4

# African Diaspora Religion

The study of African diaspora religions in the Americas is a growing field in the academy that crosses multiple interdisciplinary fields. While relying heavily on ethnography, history, and anthropology, scholars who do research in this area also combine literary studies, art history, and ritual studies in order to provide a broad picture of the complexity of African diaspora religions. The nature of their transmission, these scholars argue, requires a multi-pronged approach to their study in order to reveal the complexity of their formation in the Americas and their expressions today.

The study of African diaspora religions has methodological and theological implications. Attention to African diaspora religions decenters the overwhelming predominance of Christianity in liberationist discourses. The serious consideration of African diaspora religions, as well as other non-Christian religions in the Americas, demonstrates that liberation theologians need to widen their religious scope in order to fully understand and write about the religion of the marginalized communities they claim to represent. The methodologies employed to study African diaspora religions broaden liberation theologians' conversation partners. At the same time, the study of African diaspora religions would benefit from an engagement with theology, which rarely occurs in the field. This is a dialogue that would enrich both fields of study. It would force scholars of distinctive religious traditions to confront the presuppositions contained in the theological worldviews of the religions they study. This dialogue also opens the door for a more porous understanding of religious identity throughout the Americas.

## Decentering Christianity

A hallmark of liberation theologies has been their theological and methodological emphasis on Christianity. This focus is not surprising, given both the academic pedigrees of most liberation theologians and the unarguable predominance of Christianity in the region. However, ignoring the presence of non-Christian religions or treating them as superfluous add-ons to a Christian theological worldview greatly weakens these scholars' assessments of religion in the Americas. It disregards the multifaceted religious landscape of the Americas and does not address the impact non-Christian religions have had on Christianity itself. I assess liberation theologies through the lens of scholarship that focuses on African diaspora religions in the Americas. However, I should note that a similar chapter could be written through the lens of indigenous religions as well as the broad religious pluralism of the Americas.

The decentering of Christianity is also essential for understanding the complex manner in which Christianity arrived in the Americas. Here, I do not need to reiterate the impact of the trans-Atlantic slave trade and the genocide of indigenous peoples. However, the impact of Christianity on these populations is often understood by assessing what Christianity imported to the region. More attention needs to be paid to what Christianity also took away. "Scholars of religion must continually revisit this conversation for we are in the best position to think about not only what White orthodox Christianity has done to Black people and Black religion but also what it has taken away from Black people and Black religion."[1] Scholars should simultaneously examine what Christianity has brought to the table and the religious identities and worldviews Christianity also shoved off the table. Although it has an entirely different power dynamic, the impact of non-Christian religions on the theology and practice of Christianity is also significant.

Liberation theologies have historically ignored the substantial influence of non-Christian religions on Christianity, instead arguing for a biblically based liberationist message that is revealed in the concrete religious practices of marginalized communities. In addition to relying heavily on the Christian bible, some liberation theologians draw from the theology revealed in the popular religious practices of Christian communities, particularly in their understanding of Jesus and, in Catholic circles, Mary. These religious practices reveal moments when the encounter of Christianity and non-Christian religions creates a space where theological worldviews and symbolism intertwine. Too often the theological impact of this encounter is downplayed and a normative Christian worldview dominates.

Although this is the overwhelmingly normative paradigm, at moments serious attention to the non-Christian elements of marginalized religion is given in the theological arena. As highlighted by womanist theologian and scholar of Caribbean religion Dianne Stewart, the work of womanist theologian Delores Williams offers hints of a womanist theology that challenges a normative Christian theological agenda. This challenge is apparent in Williams' groundbreaking research on the figure of Hagar in the Hebrew Scriptures. In emphasizing Hagar, Williams disputes the normative liberationist reading of the Exodus narrative that depicts the God of the Hebrew Scriptures exclusively within a liberationist paradigm. Williams's shift inserts an African worldview into Christian liberationist interpretations of this narrative through her use of nontraditional sources and recovery of "African residuals" in the biblical text.[2] The emphasis on Hagar is an African contribution to the biblical narrative and undermines the exclusively liberationist reading of the Exodus.

Native American liberation theologians in the United States have consistently challenged the normativity of the Christian narrative within liberation theologies. Theologian Robert Warrior has argued that native people historically have had an uneasy relationship with Christianity because of different worldviews and political strategies.[3] Too often Native Americans are the object and not the subject of liberation. In order to place native peoples front and center within liberationist discourse, we must see the bible through Canaanite eyes. Reading the text through native eyes reveals that Yahweh in the Hebrew Scriptures is not a liberator but a God that is a Conqueror. In the Exodus narrative, after the Hebrew liberation from Egyptian slavery, the Hebrews are commanded by Yahweh to enter the promised land and to annihilate its indigenous people. Although historical and archeological evidence tells us today that they were not annihilated, the conquest narrative remains the same. Reading the bible as well as the entire Christian corpus through native eyes decenters the exclusively Christian liberationist narrative. Critically examining the Exodus narrative in all its complexity has concrete historical implications, as is seen in the U.S. appropriation of the Canaanite conquest through Manifest Destiny.

In addition to womanist and Native American theologians, African theologians also contribute to the decentering of Christianity by highlighting the uneasy relationship with Christianity on the African continent, given the legacy of colonialism.[4] African theology arose to combat the imposed European ideal and to resist a European domination that highlights the contradiction of the European impact on Africa: the internal victimization and self-hatred of African people. African theology is a reaction to Christian European colonialism and its internalized oppressions among African peoples; it embraces an affirmation of Africa characterized by political and cultural resistance. Those scholars who emphasize culture highlight the Christian symbol as a symbol of Europe. They point to the Africanization and indigenization of Christian faith and affirm the worth of African culture. In highlighting African religion, they study, among other expressions, the African independent-church movement and African traditional / indigenous religions. African theologians who emphasize political resistance share similar concerns with black liberation theologians in the United States.

Liberation theologies that highlight the non-Christian elements within their communities demonstrate that the role of Christianity within liberation theologies should be problematized. Scholars who work in the field of African diaspora religions also challenge this Christian normativity implicitly by focusing their research on the way in which these religions contribute to the history, identity, and politics of the Americas: "Afro-Catholic religious syncretism forces Europeanized Christianity to relearn its dogma and its pastoralism. Far from [being] a deformation of true Christianity, syncretism functioned as a brake on the Catholic ideological hegemony of the time of slavery."[5] In demonstrating the complexity of religious worldviews, these scholars highlight the manner in which Christianity and African diaspora religions bleed into each other, at times forming new religious traditions, at other moments shifting the rituals and theologies of established traditions. In a similar vein, the methodology of these scholars expands the approach to the study of religion.

## The Study of African Diaspora Religion

African diaspora religions in the Americas have an African core of traditional religion that has been layered with Roman Catholicism, indigenous religions, and/or folk Catholicism. The very nature of these religious traditions challenges static definitions of religious identity. The mixture of religious beliefs and practices occurred during the trans-Atlantic slave trade and in the colonial era, when slaves had to hide their religious practices behind a Roman Catholic veneer. This self-preservation led to the incorporation of non-African elements into religious practices. The influences of these non-African diaspora religions are debated and vary not only from religion to religion but also internally within different religious communities.[6] Perhaps the two most well known of these religions is Vodou in Haiti and Santería in Cuba. These religions not only are the most studied but are also quintessential examples of the complexity of the American religious landscape. Many practitioners of these religions also self-identify as Roman Catholic, highlighting a multifaceted religiosity.

*The Loas*

Vodou is arrived in Haiti through the trans-Atlantic slave trade. A mixture of various African traditional religions, Vodou is often characterized as a religion of survival because of its instrumental role in preserving African identity and empowering enslaved Africans during French colonial rule. The name *Vodou* is in many ways a misnomer, for it is a colonial label given by the French to the religion of enslaved peoples. These groups' religious traditions (Fon, Yoruba, and Congo) intermingled and became the foundation of a new, African-derived religion, namely Vodou, which also draws on Catholicism and indigenous religion. Vodou has survived in Haiti despite numerous attempts to illegalize and marginalize it since the arrival of slaves. In 1685, the Code Noir was passed to affirm the orthodoxy of Catholicism on the island. The clergy wholeheartedly supported the Code and in addition passed various regulations to squelch African "superstition." At the core of Vodou practice is serving the spirits, known as *loas,* supernatural beings who mediate practitioners' relationships with the sacred. Practitioners have a reciprocal relationship with these *loas,* who, during the colonial period in Haiti, became syncretized with Roman Catholic images, primarily of saints and Mary, in order to mask their African roots. Slaves transfigured Roman Catholic symbols, absorbing them into their beliefs, and at times also incorporating Roman Catholic rituals into their religious practices.

Vodou has had a tumultuous effect on Haitian history and identity. This narrative begins with Bois Caïman, where a gathering of hundreds of slaves took place in August 1791 under the leadership of a man named

Dutty Boukman. The story recounts the sacrifice of animals and the evocation of African *loas*; ultimately, this ritual is the symbolic beginning of the Haitian revolution. For a long time, this was a central unifying narrative in Haitian history. Since the 1990s, however, this narrative has been challenged by Evangelical Christian missionaries who claim that, because the appeal was to African spirits and not to Jesus Christ, Boukman and his followers initiated a pact with the devil: "Moreover, to this very day, Haitians who continue Afro-Creole traditional religious practices 'ratify' that initial 'covenant' every time they address the spirit world. It is this terrible diplomatic deal and its ongoing activation that explains the downward political and economic spiral of the country."[7] This racist interpretation of Haitian history dismantles a national moment of pride and labels all African religions demonic.

The vilification of Vodou is not new. The Catholic Church has a long history of equating Vodou with demonic activity in Haiti. Campaigns by the Church against superstition, undertaken in 1896, 1913, and 1941, directly targeted Vodou practitioners and sacred sites. President Fabre Nicolas Geffrard (1859–1867) negotiated the 1860 Concordat with the Vatican that ended its schism with Haiti. As the anthropologist Kate Ramsey rightfully argues, the Church's primary role became combatting superstition. After the signing of the Concordat, popular religious practices in Haiti declined, and the Church instituted numerous sanctions against those who participated in any "magical" practices.[8] Nonetheless, given many practitioners' use of Roman Catholic elements and prayers, as well as their self-identifying as Roman Catholic and as practitioners, Roman Catholicism and Vodou coexisted in the lives of believers in spite of the institutional Church's attempts to divorce the two. As anthropologist Karen McCarthy Brown vividly recounts in her description of the First Communion ceremony of a relative of her informant, Mama Lola, many Vodou practitioners have two-tier celebrations to mark religious rites of passage: "Upstairs was the Christian event. There was a huge table loaded with food, and in the midst of it, a family Bible placed next to a cake baked in the shape of an open Bible. To acknowledge the diversity among her guests, Mama Lola arranged to have both Catholic and Protestant prayers offered before the meal. But only some of the people upstairs were invited down to the basement, where a smaller table allowed the Vodou spirits to share in the day's feast."[9] This two-tier structure is not foreign to many Haitians on the island and in the diaspora. However, although many practitioners of Vodou were comfortable with the dual structure of Roman Catholic and Vodou belief, more recent conversions to Protestantism have led to the demonization of Vodou.

Evangelicals have constructed an anti-Vodou and anti-Catholic narrative that defines their Christian path as the only one for Haiti's ultimate salvation. The historical moment for this change is ironic, for, as it becomes a globalized religion Vodou is much more visible and institutionalized than ever. The impact of globalization on Vodou is profound and has led to efforts to centralize the religion. Yet, in the process of being organized, Vodou is slowly being Christianized. A "Vodou Church" is emerging that is influenced by Christian ecclesiological structures.[10] Vodou churches are emerging that begin to look much more like their Christian counterparts than the Vodou house temples of the past.

Although contemporary approaches to studying Vodou are significant, the history of the religion also has an impact on Christian theology today. Christian theologians have inherited a tradition of vilifying traditional African religions. Vodou is often presented as the quintessential example of demonic religion in the Americas. Theologians need to confront the manner in which Christian churches and Christian theology have supported and promoted the marginalization of Vodou and, as a result, have reinforced systematic attempts to smother African religions throughout the Americas. Similarly, the emergence of Vodou demonstrates the manner in which Afro-Latin Americans established a hybrid religious identity, one that drew from and embraced multiple religious identities. The line between Christian and non-Christian, Vodou teaches us, is not so clear.

*The Orishas*

Yoruban Orisha traditions are the most extensive and celebrated African religions in the West. Their influence goes well beyond the narrowly conceived realm of the religious and saturates the secular as well, particularly through cultural production.[11] One of the gifts of the Yoruba tradition has been its ability to adapt to a new environment and to ensure the continuity of beliefs. This capability is seen, most obviously, in the tradition's survival during the trans-Atlantic slave trade and is also visible in the its adjustment since its arrival in the Americas as it is embraced by different populations.[12] The Yoruba religion arrived in Cuba relatively late in the colonial era, during the sugar boom on the island during the nineteenth century. Two events led to the mass arrival of Yoruba in nineteenth-century Cuba: the Haitian revolution, which ended European control over the most lucrative (at the time) sugar-plantation system, and infighting that was dismantling the Yoruba empire. The increase in demand for slaves occurred just as the Oyo Empire was declining.[13] This infighting and eventual collapse created fertile ground for the European exploitation of these African peoples.

Yoruba religion in Cuba is popularly known as Santería, which is problematic for many practitioners. Because it is translated as "way of the saints," there is a sense that this designation excessively emphasizes the Roman Catholic elements of this religion; these elements are uniformly seen as symbolic layers on what is understood to be at its core an African religion. *Lucumí religion* is the term often used by scholars and practitioners, even though the name *Lucumí* emerges in Cuba as a Spanish designation for Yoruban peoples and those whom the Spanish felt had regional and cultural similarities to the Yoruba.[14] Anthropologist Mercedes Cros Sandoval argues that Regla Lucumí is the most appropriate name for Santería because practitioners use *Lucumí* to refer to themselves and their language.[15] Cros Sandoval notes that there is no standardization within Santería practice and no priestly hierarchy. Groups, therefore, can differ widely. What they share is the worship of the orishas. This differentiation is also regional. Havana is very much influenced by the religion of the Oyo empire; in Matanzas, the practices of the Arará (a minority group) dominate. Perhaps the most appropriate name for the religion is Regla de Ocha (rule of ocha or orishas) because devotion to the orishas is central to the religious practice and worldview within the religion.

The Yoruba believe in a supreme being that is manifested in three entities: Olofi has a relationship with the orishas and humans; Olodumare represents natural and elemental law; Olorun is the life-giving, energizing force and is represented by the sun. Olofi created the world and humanity. We are incapable of having a direct relationship with Olodumare: instead we have a relationship with the orishas. Olorun is the material manifestation of the other two. These three entities are nothing like the Trinity; they are natural forces. The creator, Olofi, retreats from the world for he is tired of humanity and the orishas' disobedience.

Orishas can be most simply defined as superhuman beings or spirits that are worshipped in shrines through a priesthood.[16] Ultimately, they are the expression of Olodumare in this world. They are anthropomorphic manifestations of various dimensions of the natural world or expressions of particularities of the human character or both. Slaves worshipped the orishas behind the images of Catholic saints. These religious brotherhoods, also described as mutual aid societies, created a space for the preservation and survival of African religion in Cuba. The saints are not to be confused cosmologically with the orishas, although over the years the orishas have come to be integrated with the saints. Orishas have an extensive mythology; the stories are known as *patakis*.

Fundamental to Yoruba beliefs is the presence of *ashé*, "the animating force that moves both earth and cosmos. It can be found in a plant, an animal, a stone, a body of water, a hill, the heavens, the stars. But *ashé* is also present in human beings, and can be manifested through bodily actions, but is especially active in words."[17] Within Yoruba religion, barriers between the natural and the supernatural do not exist. *Ashé* saturates all aspects of the material world, including plant, animal, and inanimate materials. Plants contain *ashé* and are used ritualistically. The presence of *ashé* on altars is directly linked to soup tureens with *otanes* (sacred rocks that contain the spiritual energy of the orishas). Initiates also receive *ashé* when they are possessed by their orisha. *Ashé* is fundamental to the manner in which practitioners view the cosmos and plays a primary role in rituals—for example, divination. Possession by one's orisha, a religious ritual every initiate participates in, is a fundamental way of communing with one's orisha. These possessions take place within the boundaries of ritual. Possession also allows the orishas to commune with the human world.

In her essay examining the liberation theological themes in orisha traditions in the West, Stewart is careful to caution that these traditions do not share a theological agenda with Christianity. "African religion is not primarily oriented toward responding to social suffering. On the other hand, African religion has all the ingredients of liberation thought and praxis."[18] Although a liberation theology is not extensively present, there is a communal praxis as a result of created alternative spaces that affirm communal, cultural, linguistic, and religious values. Orisha practitioners drew from Christianity in order to protect their religion from Spanish persecution. They demonstrated the compatibility of Christianity and orisha religion, contesting the notion that their beliefs were merely barbaric superstition. In addition to the incorporation of African elements, one finds cross-fertilization of African religious practices in Cuba. Known as *reglas,* rules, the various African diaspora religions on the island are distinctive yet also interconnected. "Although orthodoxies have attempted to keep the *reglas* separate, many houses have blended and borrowed attributes from among the several systems, leading to highly syncretic or 'crossed' (*cruzado*) practices."[19] These practices influence and borrow from each other.

Another layer that is added to the Afro-Cuban religious mix is of Espiritismo, or Spiritism. Espiritismo arrived in Cuba (and other parts of the Caribbean and Latin America) through Allan Kardec's spiritual teachings, which were imported from France by elite populations. These teachings were ultimately disseminated into the broader population and mixed with folk Catholicism and African diaspora religions. Espiritismo is the belief in the presence of the spirits and in their ability to communicate with and influence the human realm. These spirits can range from personally known family members to historical figures; they communicate with the human world through mediums who are able to interact with spirits. Spirits protect human beings but can also bring them harm.[20] The influence of Espiritismo on Santería is seen in the practices of mediumship and in masses for the dead. A Christian-based Espiritismo also exists in Cuba. Religions like Santería open avenues into the complexity of Caribbean and, consequently, American religious identity. They demonstrate that one cannot exclusively study Christianity as a window into historical and contemporary religion throughout the Americas. Although the roots of Santería and Vodou are in Africa, their impact goes well beyond the Afro-Caribbean population. The extent of their impact calls for a complex approach in studying these religions.

## Methodology

The study of African diaspora religions requires an interdisciplinary framework. Scholars who work on these religious traditions form a loose collective based on what they study not necessarily how they study it. The subject, not the method, unites these voices. In spite of their methodological diversity, one method that does unite them is the substantial use of ethnography, which is seen across the board in studies of African diaspora communities throughout the Americas. A significant number of studies also take literature as a starting point for research on African diaspora communities.[21] The purpose of this section is not to argue that theologians need to mimic the methodology of these scholars. Instead, the hope is that these scholars will provide insight and direction into the ways in which liberation theologians can expand their methodological conversation partners as well as strengthen their theological claims with on-the-ground research.

One of the first academic treatments of Santería, by scholar of religion Joseph Murphy, sets the stage for future work on African diaspora religions. The methodology Murphy used was participant observation. "Using this method, I have supposedly participated in and observed scores of santería ceremonies. Yet I wonder now just how an observer participates and how a participant observes. The santeros that I met made it clear to me that, unless I abandoned the observation post of scholarly distance, I would never understand the mysteries of the *orishas*."[22] Murphy's study is divided in three parts. The first section is historical; the second recounts his participant observation; and the final part includes analysis. This is a common model for many scholars of African diaspora religions. They use a combination of participant observation through ethnography and couple this research with historical or archival research or both.[23]

A similar model is found in the groundbreaking work on Vodou by Karen McCarthy Brown, *Mama Lola: A Vodou Priestess in Brooklyn*.[24] This book provoked a strong reaction in the field because McCarthy Brown eventually converted to Vodou, the very religion she was studying. Both McCarthy Brown and Murphy combine traditional academic sources with their personal observations about the communities they are studying. This brand of ethnography crosses the invisible line the academy has drawn between being a witness and recorder of religious rituals and being a participant. It resonates with the methodology of scholars of lived religion who are working on contemporary Christianity. Cultural historian Carolyn Morrow Long's study of historical and contemporary shops that sell religious artifacts related to conjure, Vodou, rootwork, and hoodoo combines ethnography and archival work in a manner similar to scholars' self-described lived-religion approach.[25] For academics studying African diaspora religion, ethnography is essential, given that these religions are primarily ritually and orally transmitted. "The genre of anthropological ethnography began as an effort to understand the deeply local character of meaning and the local institutional context of collective human endeavors."[26] Research on contemporary communities needs to include on-the-ground research because of the diversity one finds within African diaspora religions, which is due to their nonhierarchical and nontextual nature.

McCarthy Brown's research opened up the possibility for practitioners of African diaspora religion to begin serious academic study of their religious traditions. This insider methodology allows practitioners to write academic studies of their own religions in order to dispel rumors about their beliefs and practices.[27] African diaspora religions have a long and rocky history of being portrayed overwhelmingly as witchcraft and/or cults. This legacy is fueled by Christian efforts to discredit these religions in order to affirm Christianity as the one authentic faith. Racism and colonialism add to the problem. With the academic study of these religious traditions, many negative stereotypes and myths have been dispelled. At the same time, in creating an academic memory of religions that have been orally and ritually transmitted, the nature of these religions is transformed, as a written narrative is created that establishes accountability and indirectly institutionalizes the religion.

The use of history and ethnography in researching the complexity and hybridity of African diaspora religions at times challenges these disciplines.[28] The diversity one finds in communities, the Roman Catholic elements that are present, and the cross-fertilization of African diaspora religions, all create a complex religious picture that is not easily reduced to traditional academic categories. Anthropologist Stephen Palmié emphasizes this quality in his study of Afro-Cuban religion: "Although I will tell a number of stories, aiming for the comprehensive narrative closure of a historical monograph would, to my idea, compromise the very intent of this book by imparting a sense of transparency to what I want to show is deeply problematic. So would, in my view, an expository strategy modeled after traditional social-scientific conventions of adducing case material to render plausible an overarching theoretical argument purporting to explain a certain—in this case historical—sector of reality."[29] One cannot create simple, reductionist accounts of these religions and compartmentalize them in one academic theory. The opacity of African diaspora religions must not be approached in a reductive manner by academics.

The incorporation of anthropology and ethnography into the study of African diaspora religion has a strong historical basis in the first half of the twentieth century. Mercedes Cros Sandoval's significant study of Santería also integrates ethnography and history; she situates her work in the legacy of Afro-Cuban religious ethnographers Fernando Ortiz, Rómulo Lachatañeré, and Lydia Cabrera. Cros Sandoval argues that these scholars created the field of Afro-Cuban religion through their research in Cuba. They set the stage for future research on these religions. Although all three have been criticized by contemporary scholars for the manner in which they wrote about these religions, their methodological input remains. Their work should be contextualized in light of the 1920s' surge in Afro-Cuban studies, most notably the Afrocubanismo movement. The roots of Afrocubanismo are multiple, yet one of its starting points was a reaction to the work of white scholars; it rejected their liberal, assimilationist approach to Afro-Cuban religion and culture, an approach found in the early work of Ortiz and in more conservative efforts to erase African culture in Cuba. Although figures such as Ortiz represent the birth of Afro-Cuban studies on the island, Afrocubanismo was a reaction to imperialist white scholarship on the Afro-Cuban community. Ortiz viewed Afro-Cuban culture and religion as something that must be eliminated or erased, but Cabrera, also white, celebrated Afro-Cuban cultures and religions, and a major emphasis in her corpus is the manner in which Afro-Cuban religions permeate Cuban culture and identity as whole, regardless of one's skin tone.

One element that stands out regarding much contemporary research on African diaspora religion in the Americas is its intentional separation from Latin American and Caribbean studies as a whole. Scholars working on African diaspora religion consider their research distinct from the study of Latin American and Caribbean religion, even many of the people in the communities that they study in the United States are from this region. This separation is clearly seen, for example, in the establishment of a group on African diaspora religion in the American Academy of Religion. This is a necessary field of inquiry, yet it is troubling that there seems to be a move to separate rather than to unite scholarship on the region. And although many scholars in the field of African Diaspora religion acknowledge the legacy of Cabrera and Ortiz, they do not place themselves within the tradition of Afro-Cuban ethnography. I find this distressing on two fronts. First, the move to shift the study of African diaspora religions out of Latin American and Caribbean studies appears to disassociate contemporary scholarship with its historical legacy and its contemporary allies. Second, and this mirrors concerns raised early on in the book, this move appears to be a product of the religious studies–theology divide, given that many associate scholarship on Latin American religion exclusively with theology.

Ethnography and anthropology are not the only tools used by scholars of African diaspora religion. *Òsun across the Waters: A Yoruba Goddess in Africa and the Americas* presents an excellent multidisciplinary and multicontextual study of the orisha Oshun.[30] The book contains articles on hair plaiting, mythology, history, aesthetics, and musicology. The fact that the study is a globalized approach to Oshun is also significant because it demonstrates the presence of Yoruban religion not only across the Americas but also across the globe. Ethnographic studies of Santería move well beyond field studies; they have, for example, also examined the manner in which Santería functions in medical healing.[31] Perhaps one of the most comprehensive approaches to the study of Afro-Cuban religions has been the fieldwork conducted by the African Atlantic Research Team. Team members, led by sociologist Jualynne Dodson, conduct fieldwork as participant observers at various sites in conjunction with historical research.[32] This research undermines the assumption that Afro-Cuban religion is monolithically Yoruban in origin, a stereotype that is easily perpetuated given the excess of scholarship that focuses primarily on la Regla de Ocha.[33]

In addition to the approaches mentioned above, aesthetics also plays a significant role in the study of African diaspora religion. David Brown offers an "ethnoaesthetic and ethnohistorical treatment" of Abakuá ritual arts.[34] His is the first English-language monograph to discuss the Abakuá, a secretive male religious society in Cuba. His use of ethnography and history are entry points into his analysis of the role of aesthetics (cloths, banners, costumes, and altars) and symbol among the Abakuá. Brown deftly traces the histories of these objects from their ritual life in Abakuá lodges, to their seizure by police when elitist fear fueled the persecution of the Abakuá, to their transformation into national folk art in post-Castro Cuba. His narrative parallels the life of this religion in Cuba. His close study of these aesthetic objects, particularly those that emerge from Roman Catholicism, demonstrates that their role in much more subtle and, at times, personal ways than is often implied in broad studies of syncretism in Afro-Cuban religions. Brown's later book on Santería is a detailed historical depiction of the religion that reconciles the history of art with ethnographic anthropology and archival research. Brown's text, written from the perspective of art history, ethnography, and anthropology, offers a vivid and textured portrayal of Santería, emphasizing the artistic and ritualized dimensions of this often-misunderstood religion.[35] Using a combination of archival data, case studies, and oral narrative, Brown has written a definitive study of Afro-Cuban religion. Brown depicts Afro-Cuban religion's resilience as an active struggle in an often-hostile world and not mere passive acceptance in order to survive. "The . . . religions in Cuba were creatively and selectively reorganized in settings of 'encounter' in which African practices were conserved, as well as transformed, through processes of innovation and 'culture building,' entailing what some have called syncretism and creolization."[36] This is, in essence, the thesis of the book. Brown's emphasis is on religion as a process involving practice, performance, and public ritual.

An aesthetic approach to the study of Santería is also found in the edited volume *Santería Aesthetics in Contemporary Latin American Art*.[37] The book intertwines multidisciplinary approaches to the study of Santería—like myth, oral history, and anthropology—with essays in the field of art history. The emphasis on aesthetics also expands to the study of music and literature.[38] Scholars working in the field of Afro-Cuban aesthetics focus on art, literature, narrative, and ritual as foundational components of the Afro-Cuban religious worldview. They also are keys for understanding the function of race in the construction of religious and national identity in Cuba. Myth and narrative become transmitters of religious identity and religious knowledge.[39] Mythology becomes a source of ritual knowledge.

Although these approaches offer a rich depiction of the landscape of diaspora religion, they often lack a substantial theological analysis. Many of these texts offer a descriptive account of these religions, both historically and in the contemporary context. They give substantial historical accounts of the founding and development of these religions. And, when addressing the contemporary context, they offer a colorful tapestry of practitioners and religious leaders and of the manner in which their religious beliefs empower them to negotiate their everyday lives and struggles. However, little attention has been paid to the theological worldview that informs these religions. This focus is especially vital when one considers the impact of Catholicism, in particular, on these religious worldviews. Although many studies have examined the manner in which Roman Catholic prayers and iconography have influenced African diaspora religions, the manner in which Catholicism has theologically shaped these religions has yet to be seriously examined. This would be a substantial contribution theologians could make to the study of African diaspora religions. A study of the theological import of Catholicism would also shed light on the manner in which these religions become particularly American religious expressions in the diaspora. I am well aware of the debate between practitioners and scholars on the impact of Catholicism on the worldview, theology, and iconography of African diaspora religions. Although I agree that the original role of Roman Catholic images was to serve as a mask for African religion, eventually this mask became incorporated as an expression of African religion, particularly as seen in the loas and orishas.

Babalú-Ayé is the orisha of illnesses and plagues, especially skin ailments. Devotees of Babalú-Ayé, when possessed by this orisha, dance with the movements of a sick man, moving with gestures that exhibit pain. Like the Cuban "Saint" Lazarus, with whom he is syncretized, Babalú-Ayé limps on a crutch and is surrounded by dogs that lick his open wounds. Babalú-Ayé is able to both cure and inflict disease. Devotees often pray to him for protection against illnesses and diseases. The association of Babalú-Ayé with crutches symbolically demonstrates his association with Lazarus. Also, as Afro-Cuban scholar Eugenio Matibag argues, the "softening" of the orisha, who has Lazarus's qualities of humility and gentleness, demonstrates how attributes of a Roman Catholic saint are transferred to an orisha.[40] The attributes of Babalú Ayé have been modified by his arrival in Cuba and his association with a Roman Catholic image. Although studies that examine the relationship between the loas, the orishas, and the saints often emphasize the influence of African religious worldviews on the Roman Catholic images, much more work needs to be done examining the impact of Roman Catholicism on the theological constructions of the loas and the orishas.

## Linking Theology and African Diaspora Religions

Scholars who focus on African diaspora religions in the Americas are forced to employ an interdisciplinary approach to study this complex religious landscape in order to truly account for its diversity. Yet one area that these scholars rarely engage is theology and, more important, liberation theologies. In connecting the study of African diaspora religions

with liberation theologies I am not alone. Stewart calls for "an appropri-
able research model for womanist studies of pre-emancipation African
diasporic religious formation."

> How would womanist discourse about slavery change if more regional
> and local studies analyzed African diasporic experience with refer-
> ence to the actual African ethnic populations that were enslaved within
> specific geographic regions in America? Dialoguing with scholars in
> African diaspora studies, whose research on specific African and Afri-
> can-American peoples with direct cultural linkages, provides a sound
> scholarly basis for developing competent theologies that resonate with
> the nuances of the African heritage in the African diasporic experience.
> It also strengthens the credibility of our scholarship by replacing specu-
> lative questions about the African heritage in the African diaspora with
> tangible data from which to draw sources for constructive womanist
> God-talk.[41]

Stewart acknowledges the legacy of Christianity for African Americans, yet argues persuasively that the study of African diaspora religions
challenges the assumptions of black-liberation and womanist theologies about black religious identity. These assumptions are based on a
construction of black religious identity that is witnessed exclusively in a
Christian context.[42] In addition, the study of African diaspora religions
forces scholars to explore what is African about African American Christianity. Even scholars who choose to focus their research exclusively on
African American Christianity will benefit from a more nuanced understanding of the Christianity of enslaved Africans.

Stewart's own scholarship centers on the theological analysis of
Jamaican women who take part in Kumina, a religious ceremony.[43]
Stewart incorporates ethnographic research, history, and womanist
theological categories into her analysis of African diaspora religion,
demonstrating that theological analysis can enrich the study of African
diaspora religions. Stewart begins by outlining the history of Kumina

in Jamaica; she then examines the importance of the category of "Africanness" to their culture and religion and applies the multidimensional analysis of womanism to the role of the women within Kumina. Hers is a communal approach that relies heavily on sociocultural analysis. Too often these religions are reduced to folk culture in Jamaica through public rituals and dances. Stewart's emphasis is on the religious validity of Kumina in Jamaican history and in conversation with womanist thought.

Theologian Maricel Mena López also calls for the incorporation of African diaspora religions into Christian theological discourse, particularly in Latin America. "The Latin American Afro-feminist Theology (TAFLA) we describe here springs, then, from the need to create theology from experiences of community and religious life, of women of Christian faith, and women of faiths of African origin in Latin America and the Caribbean. The theology is concerned first and foremost with the situations of racism, sexism, classism, colonialism, and anti-semitism which mark the life experiences of the oppressed in our societies."[44] This theological perspective does not just end with the inclusion of poor black women into theological discourse. Instead, poor black women become the subjects of theology as epistemological agents; the inclusion of black women's voices is a methodological feature.

Theologians are not the only scholars of religion who are finding avenues to connect liberation theologies with African diaspora religions. A liberationist interpretation of Vodou is found in Deborah O'Neil and Terry Rey's study of devotion to St. Philomena in northern Haiti. In the Haitian devotion to St. Philomena she has sacred power. She gives what O'Neill and Rey describe as a liberation hagiography that emphasizes survival, resistance, and self-determination. In a similar manner to the function of the preferential option for the poor in liberation theology, "*liberation hagiography* is motivated by the conviction that Catholic saints exercise just such a preferential option, as is so clearly on display among St. Philomena's devotees in Haiti."[45] Her relationship with the Vodou loa Lasyrenn demonstrates the manner in which Catholicism and Vodou enrich each other. The authors, who define popular religious practices as expressions of liberation theology, connect the demise of liberation theology in Haiti to the deterioration of the cult of the saints. Their study offers a significant contribution to this conversation. On the one hand, their criticism of liberation theology's inability to connect with lived religious expressions is sound. On the other hand, they open up the field of liberation hagiography to the study of American religion as a whole. Research on liberation hagiography is a much-needed avenue of study that would unite concrete investigations of religious devotions with liberationist movements and studies of African diaspora religions.

Rey rightfully points out in his own study of the cult of the Virgin Mary that Catholicism in Haiti is marked by Marian devotion.[46] The same can be said of Mexican and Cuban Catholicism, as well of Catholicism in many other countries in the Americas.[47] Columbus, Rey points out, arrived in the Americas on the Santa María and named the first two ports in Hispaniola after Mary. I would add devotion to saints and folks saints as another defining element of Catholicism in the Americas. Although Mariology in particular has been a wellspring of liberationist impulses, it has also been a source of misogyny and oppression. Devotion to Mary is also not exclusively found in the realm of the poor but crosses class lines. However, the Mary of the poor bears little resemblance to the Mary of the rich. The notion of liberation hagiography introduces a fruitful avenue for exploring the connection between lived religious practices and liberationist impulses in Marian and other folk devotions, particularly among the disenfranchised. Such an analysis should examine not only symbol and culture but also class and power in Christian, indigenous, and African religions.

A conversation among liberation theologians throughout the Americas and scholars of African diaspora religion would both challenge and strengthen each field of study. Liberation theologians would confront a religious world that is different from their own Christo-centric vision of the religion of the marginalized. They would also become privy to studies that demonstrate the complexity of the religious landscape they are researching. Scholars of African diaspora religion would benefit from the insights, both Christian and non-Christian, that theologians could bring to the conversation. In addition, through a broad dialogue between religious studies and theology, both discourses would be forced to face the fact that the manner in which religious, racial, and cultural identity has been constructed in their own fields has been limited by their research emphases.

# Conclusion

This book opened with a discussion of the contested relationship between theology and religious studies in the contemporary academy. This debate has plagued scholars for decades, and no apparent resolution seems to be on the horizon. The study of religion itself remains a porous field, with little agreement among scholars surrounding the object of our study (religion) and the approach that unifies our scholarship (method). The manner in which the U.S. academy uses the category of religion is overwhelmingly Western and is significantly influenced by Christianity. Theology appears to be limited largely to the study of Christianity. Adding to the conversation are debates about when the field of religion actually began. The Enlightenment and the encounter with non-Christian civilizations in the 1600s clearly opened a significant conversation that is a precursor to our field. This study was later institutionalized in the nineteenth century when university positions began to be offered on the topic of religion.

The field of religion was established with a Christian emphasis that came to view non-Christian religions as secondary and lesser. This Christian framework developed the imperialist eyes through which religion as a whole was assessed. Today, more than ever, scholars need to shed this legacy. Although scholarship from the global South and on non-Christian religions has exploded since the 1960s, Christianity remains the privileged religion in the field of religious studies. The favorable position of Christianity is seen, for example, in the joint meetings of the American Academy of Religion and the Society for Biblical Literature, and the uproar that arose when these meetings were separated. The assumption remains that Christianity is the dominant and primary object of study. The Christian-centric study of religion leads to a racist approach to non-Christian traditions, in which the religions of African and indigenous peoples are labeled as primitive.

In addition to privileging the place of Christianity, there has been an unbalanced emphasis on scholarship written by European and Euro-American scholars. They remain the dominant voice within the academy. This unbalanced perspective ignores demographics around the globe. The centers of Christianity are increasingly Latin America and Africa, not Europe. This change is of special importance for the U.S. academy, for, by 2040, racial minorities will become the majority.[1] The field of religion must take a closer look at these often understudied regions, such as Africa and Latin America, in order to understand their complex religious landscape. There exists a fluid religious identity that does not fall into the rigid categories of the academy. This fluidity also applies to the Americas as a whole, where the borders that divide North and South are much more porous than ever. The future of the study of religion must be open to the messiness of religious identity.

## Inroads of Dialogue

Can we even speak of liberation in non-Christian religions? Numerous scholars have argued that non-Christian religions contain elements of liberation, albeit with a different register than what is traditionally understood by Christianity. One point that is often reiterated is that for oppressed peoples the survival of their religious identities is a form of liberation. The ability of the Yoruban slave in Cuba, for example, to maintain his of her religious beliefs and practices, albeit in secret and in a modified manner, was a form of empowerment. The survival of religion contributes to the survival of language, culture, and social structures.[2] Similarly, those who came to accept the Christian worldview imposed on them were at times able to maintain traces of their African beliefs within their new religious framework.[3] This possibility became a form of liberation, for non-Christian religions serve as a source of hope for disenfranchised peoples. Although the message of empowerment is present, theologians need to be careful not to insert non-Christian religions into a Christian understanding of liberation.

The need for a conversation between liberation theologians and scholars of non-Christian religions in the Americas is not a novel idea; it has existed in Latin America since the mid-1980s, when scholars of black theology in Latin America and the Caribbean began coming together to talk with each other and with practitioners of non-Christian religions. Unfortunately, many of their studies are published exclusively in Spanish, thereby limiting their accessibility in the broader U.S. academy. An excellent example of this work is the volume *Cultura negra y teología*, papers from the 1984 gathering of ASETT (La Asociación de Téologos del Tercer Mundo, the Association of Third World Theologians) in San Pablo, Brazil. The goal of this gathering and the papers that were published as a result of it was to explore the diverse religious expression of Afro-Latin Americans. Participants came from all over Latin America and the Caribbean, and papers examined Vodou, liberation theology, syncretism, and Afro-Christian religious expressions. The book calls for liberation theologians to see popular religion and African diaspora religions as a resource for their work. If Christian churches and scholars do not recognize the legitimacy and value of African diaspora religions, liberation theology will never represent the faith of marginalized peoples in their regions. The U.S. academy could learn a lesson from these types of projects.[4]

Within Latin America, inroads are being made into exploring the significance of religious pluralism. This conversation is framed by the desire to understand the complexity of the Latin American religious landscape and the theological importance of religious pluralism. The starting point of this dialogue for Christians, however, must be a rejection of Christianity as the sole avenue to the sacred. God cannot be understood exclusively in Christian terms. Liberation theologians need to recognize the limitations of defining the sacred exclusively as Christian and to entertain the possibility that salvation in Christ may not be limited to Christianity. This Christian arrogance has systematically ignored the presence of the sacred in indigenous and African diaspora religions.[5] A Christianity that is rooted in its cultural context cannot identify itself as a replacement of other religious traditions. Religious traditions must share an equal place at the table. Interreligious dialogue should recognize the "interreligious communion" already occurring in the religious life of many Latin Americans. These individuals do not identify themselves as adhering to two religious traditions but instead understand their religious worldview as a synthesis. This synthesis of religious traditions is one of the greatest challenges to Christian theology today, which often wants to reduce syncretic faith to two-religion membership.[6] It is also distinct from inculturated religion, which refers to religion shaped by culture and context.

Within Latino/a theology, I am not the first to suggest this dialogue. Latino theologian Orlando Espín presents a body of work that addresses many of the concerns raised above. Since his doctoral studies, his writings have taken African diaspora religions seriously. After spending several years writing almost exclusively about Catholicism, he has now returned in his work to the impact of African diaspora religions on Christian theology. Espín proposes a Latino/a theology of religions in light of the strong presence of African diaspora and indigenous religions among Latino/as and Latin Americans. His theology of religions is one that emerges from a Christian framework that has as its roots the loving and compassionate Christian God, one that is experienced, at times unknowingly, beyond the boundaries of Christianity. He does a fine job of situating the need for this dialogue within the history of Christian intellectual thought. While I commend and agree with Espín's call to authentic dialogue with African diaspora religions, its exclusively Christian theological framework is a concern. Many practitioners of these religions would feel quite uncomfortable with the claim that "non-Christians can and do experience God's love and grace, even if they might not name, know, or explain it in a Christian manner."[7] This approach of the "anonymous Christian" is problematic and leads to a devaluing of the theological worldviews of African diaspora religions. Although, as Espín notes, Jesus Christ is the definitive revelation for Christian believers, academics do not have to maintain that claim in our research. This point raises the broader question of the role of the theologian in relationship to the Church. Is the theologian's role to promote the teachings of the Church or to reveal the complex religious beliefs of practitioners?

In Latin America, theologian Maricel Mena López calls for a symmetrical dialogue between religious traditions in the context of pluralism. This dialogue challenges religions to reject the notion that their truths are objective and universal. Liberation theologies should recognize that the current religious context transcends and dismantles the rigid borders of religious identity.[8] Mena López usefully frames this dialogue, acknowledging that the word of God can be found outside Christian Scriptures. Her proposed engagement respects the spirit of religious traditions, without one religion dominating the categories and framework of the dialogue. As a result of these conversations theological categories can be opened to more fully address the plurality of religious traditions. This dialogue will not be easy. The incorporation of non-Christian religions within liberation theologies is complicated by the different theological worldviews that these religions uphold. These conversations must take the form of a give and take, in which one is open to the challenge of other religious traditions.[9] And yet this authentic dialogue could lead to some theological roadblocks for meaningful exchange, particularly regarding the notion of salvation history.

Not every religion has a narrative of salvation history similar to that found in Christian theology. Moreover, the primacy of Christian revelation within liberation theologies poses a challenge to practitioners of non-Christian religions. Christianity's self-understanding as the exclusive religion with the special revelation of the sacred implies a condemnation of non-Christian religions, particularly of African diaspora religions in light of the trans-Atlantic slave trade. The censure of African diaspora religions has led to the exploitation of their belief systems and practitioners. Because these religions do not have a redemptive history that contains a special Christian revelation, they are viewed as lesser. This view has become increasingly apparent as Pentecostal and Evangelical Christianity spreads throughout the Americas. These expressions of Protestant Christianity, in particular, often depict African diaspora religions as demonic and evil.

The particularity of Christian revelation is not the only hurdle that needs to be overcome for dialogue to succeed. It is important to understand that African-derived religions do not assume that humans require some special redemption. Life is characterized by misfortune, and these religions are oriented toward well-being and fulfillment. The grand narrative of a liberating God is not present, which is very much at odds with the foundational theological worldview of liberation theologians. This worldview assesses the validity of a religious tradition based on how it addresses soteriology in light of historical, human liberation.[10] In other words, there is a core theological difference in the construction of salvation histories between these religions. The question for liberation theologies is whether they can interact with a theological discourse that does not connect salvation with liberation. For African diaspora religions, the challenge emerges from the question of liberation. Is the emphasis on survival and flourishing liberative in the same manner as liberation through a soteriological lens? How do these religions negotiate the question of suffering? How do they empower local communities in the face of oppression? Clear contextual examples address this issue in terms of identity, yet the question of redemption hangs over these religions.

In his excellent multidisciplinary study of the mutual-aid religious society called Abakuá, Ivor Miller demonstrates how Cross River Basin religion became a source of liberation in colonial Cuba. Abakuá lodges were able to maintain a sense of morality and history in the face of brutal slavery. "West Africans collectively refashioned an institution in the Americas, resulting in the liberation of many from slavery and strengthening the struggle for independence from a European colonial power, thus shaping the emerging nation-state in lasting ways."[11] Yet, the fact that Abakuá is depicted as providing a liberative space for West Africans does not necessarily translate into a liberationist theology. The social and political function of a religion can vary quite dramatically from its theological emphasis. We must find ways to speak of liberation outside of Christianity. This need is reflected in many discussions within Latino/a theology on the topic of popular religion. Although popular religion is understood as distinct from popular Christianity or popular Catholicism, too often scholars approach popular religion from a Christian framework, where indigenous and African practices are seen as peripheral additions to a Christian core.[12] A distinction must be maintained between the function of religion within society and its theological worldview. There should be collaborative studies of both their theological and their sociological functions because they have an impact on each other. A ritual that promotes empowerment socially may or may not be progressive theologically. Instead it may serve to reify structures of hierarchy and submission within religious structures.

## Identity

African diaspora religions are understood as empowering racially marginalized communities on the issue of identity. In maintaining African religious identity, worldviews, languages, and rituals in the face of slavery, colonialism, and neocolonialism, these religions refuse to allow the authentic African legacy in the Americas to be erased. Yet these religions go beyond mere survival. They demonstrate the theological significance of African traditional religious worldviews in the Americas. They reject the narrative of an exclusively Christian vision of historical liberation. Their study emphasizes the intersection of race, culture, class, and power in the religious landscape of the American hemisphere.

There are hints of theological resources within African diaspora religions that could be consonant with liberation theologies. The very presence of African spirits in the diaspora could offer a theological entry point into liberationist reflections. For example the *pataki* of the Yoruban *orisha* Oshun's arrival in Cuba describes her as saddened when European slave traders took so many of her children to Cuba. She thus decided to move there, having her sister Yemayá straighten her hair and lighten her skin so that all Cubans would identify with her. This myth surrounding her arrival in the diaspora reflects a theological shift in *orisha* religion to accommodate her arrival in the Americas. A study of such shifts and the transformation of Yoruban religion, among others, in the diaspora could be an important entry point for discovering liberationist impulses in their theologies. A critical question is the manner in which the theologies of these African-based religions have been affected by the conditions of slavery throughout the Americas. Oshun's *pataki* not only reveals a change in physical identity but also affirms that the *orishas* travel to Cuba not only to accompany African slaves but also potentially to enter the spiritual life of non-African Cubans. Race in this story is not solely about physical identity.

Although the topic of identity is central, liberation theologians often struggle to demonstrate the theological import of their insights on identity. Many theologians emphasize race and culture, yet in such a way that these categories become lost in debates over identity politics. An example of a corrective in this trend is found in Brian Bantum's provocative work examining biracial identity as theological. Bantum begins by challenging U.S. minority theologians to look beyond concrete embodiment when theologically reflecting on the body and, instead, to consider the body through a Christological lens emphasizing Jesus's hybridity. Racial embodiment needs to be recast as a Christological, not just a social, phenomenon. Jesus's redemption is not simply the redemption of our bodies from oppression.[13] Bantum offers a Christological anthropology based on the notion that Christ is mulatto. Jesus was human and divine; his is a personhood that emerges out of difference. "Jesus is mulatto is an ontological claim that suggests the union of flesh and Spirit is a fact of Jesus' personhood."[14] In contrast to the life of the American mulatto in the nineteenth and twentieth centuries, which was one of violence and tragedy, Jesus's *mulatez* reveals the transformative nature of hybridity. He creates a mulatto community by inviting us into a hybrid community through the Spirit. Bantum's analysis reveals the manner in which concepts such as race and identity are theological. The hybridity of Jesus's mulatto identity as human and divine also reveals an ontology of hybridity that is characteristic of religion in the Americas. Scholarship such as his pushes the question of identity into the theological realm and outside the realm of identity politics, giving the category of hybridity theological value.

Although scholars too often draw clear lines between Christian and non-Christian religions, some religious rituals also blur them. Devotion to folk saints is a clear example of this phenomenon; such devotion contains a mixture of official and folk catholicisms that occur along with devotion to canonized saints. Folk saints are spirits of the dead that can perform miracles, and most are born in Latin America. They are often connected to their communities through their national identity, class status, and geographical locality. One example of a growing devotion to a folk saint is the adulation of Santa Muerte in Mexico and the United States (particularly, though not exclusively, among Mexican Americans).[15] Santa Muerte is the only female personification of death in the Americas, unlike other folk saints of death like San La Muerte (Argentina) and Rey Pascual (Guatemala). Testimonies of her efficaciousness as a miracle worker have contributed greatly to the rapid spread of devotion to her. Her devotees are often caricatured as drug dealers and criminals, and Catholic and Protestant churches condemn her devotion. In actuality, her devotees span the diversity of the Mexican and Mexican American population. Devotees make a variety of petitions to her relating to wisdom, love, healing, and money. Roman Catholicism influences many of the rituals and imagery surrounding Santa Muerte, despite the church's claims that devotion to her is Satanic. Santa Muerte votive candles, for example, resemble official Roman Catholic votive candles to Mary and the saints. In Doña Queta's shrine to Santa Muerte in Mexico City, devotees participate in monthly modified rosary services. Masses are also said in her honor. Devotees' dedication to Santa Muerte blurs the lines between Christian and non-Christian identity in the American religious landscape, in the same way that African diaspora religions use Catholic symbolism, rituals, and prayers in their practices.

Dialogue with African diaspora religions also challenges the construction of the poor in liberation theologies. Latin American liberation theology in particular highlights the economic poor as central to the Christian message and to Christian praxis. Its emphasis on the poor is based not just on their suffering but on the seemingly privileged status given to their pious faith life and devotions. As Marcella Althaus-Reid thoughtfully points out, "Somehow, and with few exceptions, the classification of the poor in Liberation Theology became a moral category. . . . The real poor, especially poor women who did not fit the stereotypes of the church, disappeared." The poor were constructed as proper and "decent."[16] This development is due to what Althaus-Reid interprets as an ecclesiocentric depiction of the poor. She challenges the construction of the poor in liberation theology, with an emphasis on urban and gay populations. Her sound critique could usefully be broadened to include not only the many who fall out of Christian categories but also those within churches who are not seen as authentic Christians.

An interesting discussion surrounding gender would also emerge from a serious conversation between scholars of African diaspora religions and liberation theologies. Studies of Santería have noted that Santería practices often force both male and female practitioners to embrace female qualities. Men are at times compelled to adopt female roles as part of their religious practice. Conversely women are also required to move between gender roles, particularly when it comes to possession by male orishas. This code switching between gender roles reveals a fluid understanding of gender identity and the manner in which it is ritually embodied, both for the human and for the supernatural.[17] Underlying this fluidity is an understanding of gender in which women are not seen as defective males and gender is not normatively male. This fluidity is seen primarily in lived ritual life, which begs the question of the most appropriate method for understanding and academically researching these religious traditions.

## Religion in the Americas Reconceived

The field of religion today is dominated by a textualism that reduces the study of religion to mastery over books written by scholars of religion.[18] Yet one cannot detach texts from everyday life. We must look at both the discursive and the nondiscursive as embodied practices. Religious practices manifest themselves in polymorphous ways. Texts, beliefs, and symbols must be historicized and contextualized. The textual emphasis affects not only the methodology of religious studies but also its audience and sources. Liberation theologians cannot speak only to the academy; they need to become public intellectual voices. Although liberation theologies should maintain concrete connections to lived religious communities, this relationship does not have to be accomplished exclusively in ecclesial settings. Theologian James Evans describes this interconnection quite poetically when he argues that black theology "must be in touch with the 'guts' of black religion."[19] One dimension of black theology is the faith of the Black Church. However, black religious experience in the Americas is not limited to churches. Evans also calls for an embodied contextual understanding of God that is not a philosophical abstraction but is grounded in everyday lived religious practices and beliefs. His comments apply to liberation theologies as a whole.

One of the hallmarks of liberation theologies has been their dialogue with the social sciences. This emphasis on social science has led to a broader engagement with society as whole, but not at the grassroots level. Liberation theologians speak of structural social issues, yet they do not focus sufficiently on everyday religion. Methodologically, this kind of approach involves theoretical borrowing for theology from other fields. Yet liberation theology can fruitfully turn to the social sciences not only to offer an analysis of the broader social picture but also to examine concrete, localized religion.[20] Theology needs to move into the study of lived religion, drawing from ethnography and cultural studies. Nancy Pineda-Madrid's book on social suffering and salvation offers an excellent example of the type of on-the-ground research that can expand contemporary liberation theologies. Beginning her text with a thick description of feminicide in Juárez, Mexico, she does not approach women's suffering in abstraction but as an embodied, contextual reality.[21] And yet an emphasis on lived religion does not have to be at the expense of texts. Instead, cultural studies and ethnography must always be in dialogue with textual approaches to the study of religion.[22] One cannot rely exclusively on a textual approach in order to arrive at the core of religious experience and identity, but, on the flip side, one cannot give only descriptive accounts of religion. Theological analyses of the faith lives of practitioners need to remain a significant dimension of the study of religion.[23] We cannot look only at everyday religion in isolated instances. We should also contextualize these studies in light of broader theological currents. One needs to situate material religion within the broader theological worldview that both shapes and is shaped by it. One should feed the other; textual studies must be accompanied by research of concrete communities with a balance of the two, for they complement each other.

Perhaps the greatest correction scholars who focus on the religion of marginalized peoples in the Americas need to make is to stop referring to the religious context of the past and to engage the present instead. The world that gave rise to Latin American liberation theology, for example, is dramatically different today. Liberation theology arose in a time when revolutionary action marked the Latin American landscape. This was an optimistic time in which the poor and marginalized were seen as agents of social change. The polarization of capitalism and socialism also marked this time period.[24] In a similar vein black liberation theology needs to stop referring to the civil rights and black power movements as grassroots sources for liberation theology today. Instead, it needs to focus on grassroots ecclesial and social movements of the present. Latino/a theologians should recognize the religious and demographic diversity of their communities and acknowledge the academic, not ecclesial, audience for their scholarship. Liberation theology today must not perpetuate the forty-year-old writings of its founders. It needs to respond to contemporary issues in light of its original ethical-political critique. The new subjects of liberation theology include women, indigenous peoples, Afro-American peoples, and forgotten religious traditions.[25]

These new subjects will challenge liberation theologies as a whole, particularly in light of the dominant Christian tradition. Liberation theologians do not tend to read the bible as being situated in the contemporary context in all its complexity. The Exodus paradigm, adopted by so many liberation theologians, for example, must be interpreted by recognizing that the narrative vilifies the Canaanites and begins with the rape and banishment of Hagar. Black liberation theologians lift the Exodus story up as paradigmatic for both liberation narratives in the Hebrew Scriptures and the nature of God.[26] This narrative, while recounting the liberation of the Hebrews from slavery, is far from paradigmatic for liberation as a whole. One cannot ignore that the Exodus narrative is followed by the conquest of the Canaanites. The broad narrative of the Exodus should be studied in its fullness. Yes, it contains the liberation of the Hebrews from Egyptian slavery. However it is a narrative that privileges one group over the other. Liberation is not available to everyone.[27] To claim that the Exodus narrative is liberationist is to deny its bias. God is not always clearly a liberator for everyone. Christian translation of the Exodus narrative into a liberationist narrative should also examine the dehumanizing character of slavery in New Testament times. The Christian Scriptures do not contain a comprehensive condemnation of slavery, and scholars often deemphasize the corporality of slavery and the sexual vulnerability of slaves at the hands of their slave masters.[28] Additionally, liberation theologians have not sufficiently addressed global capitalism and its impact on the poor throughout the world.

Liberationist interpretations of the Exodus are linked to a broader social-location hermeneutics—reading the bible with one's social location as the point of departure—that dominates contemporary liberation theologies. Although social-location hermeneutics is significant for liberation theology's method, it also has its limitations. Too often social-location hermeneutics is used to legitimize the contemporary community that is placed into the narrative.[29] Social-location hermeneutics does not challenge the biblical tradition's authority and is used to confirm the otherness of marginalized peoples. The otherness a scholar wants to privilege (race, culture, gender) becomes synonymous with marginalization within the biblical text.[30] The otherness remains unchallenged and in fact becomes legitimized by the biblical tradition.

In many ways liberation theologians have lost their path. They are engaging not the religion of the present but instead a romanticized version of the religion of the past. Liberation theologians have a responsibility to acknowledge the areas in which they have been too myopic when looking at the Christian tradition, the communities they claim to represent, and the presence of non-Christian religions.[31] Liberation theologians have oversimplified the complexity of oppressed peoples and outright ignored certain people. More important, however, these scholars have an ethical responsibility to correct their oversights. This critique is not exclusive to liberation theologians, but in claiming to represent the marginalized in their writings they have opened themselves up to criticism of the manner in which they have created "ontological oppression" in their writings.

In spite of their shortcomings, one cannot deny that liberation theologies are plagued by exaggerated expectations of their historical possibilities. These possibilities are not only sociological but also theological. Brazilian theologian Jung Mo Sung describes the liberationist vision as the Exodus paradigm within liberation theology, as seeing God's justice enacted at the center of human history, in contrast to the Christian worldview that acknowledges the limits of human history. The crucified Christ reveals that God does not undo human history. In other words, the core of the Christian message is not the triumph of Exodus. The Christian core is the crucified Christ, the suffering servant. The paradox of the cross reminds us that the struggle against oppression is not a hero's story but one that will be marked by, and continue in spite of, struggle and setbacks.[32] This is a provocative and significant insight. Liberation theology should not be theologically about the victory; instead it needs to be about the struggle. This insight could revitalize the work of contemporary scholars in the contemporary globalized world.

The narratives of African diaspora religions have also been transformed since the 1980s. One clear example is the revisionist history of Bois Caïman, the iconic Vodou ritual. For centuries, this ritual was seen as the catalyst for the Haitian revolution, thus linking Vodou to the emancipation of Haitians from slavery and their independence from French colonial rule. Evangelical Christians have recast this story as being about a pact made by slaves with the devil, unwittingly making Satan the ruler of Haiti.[33] The existence of Vodou on the island, they argue, continues to renew this covenant. Vodou becomes the reason for Haiti's suffering, a force that needs to be eradicated in order for Haiti to flourish spiritually and materially. Increasingly Vodou is seen as a threat to, not a part of, Haiti's future.

Critiques of African diaspora religions do not emerge solely from a Christian context but also among practitioners of various religious traditions. The historical and contemporary dynamic among African diaspora religions needs to be critically examined. For example, in order to gain increased acceptance in Cuban culture as a whole, Yoruba orisha cults in Cuba scapegoated Congolese *nganga* practices to make their own religious practices more acceptable. By vilifying the religious traditions of the Congolese, they were able to recast their religious practices as the most authentic and least threatening African on the island.[34] These two "religions" were caricatured as distinct "ritual idioms": one focusing on reciprocity, the other on labor and payment. The stereotypes of these religions allow one to be more ritually acceptable, especially as Afro-Cuban religions become tapped as a source of Afro-Cuban folklore in

a post-Castro retrieval of Cuban identity as Afro-Latin. This development is seen in the ritual idioms of these religions as well. Although
practitioners of Santería often prominently display their ritual objects in
their homes, practitioners of Congolese religions tend to hide their ritual
objects. This dynamic reveals that issues of power and acceptability mark
the Afro-Cuban religious landscape internally and that the landscape is
not merely a polarized dynamic between Christians and non-Christians.
The historical and contemporary worlds of these religions are much more
complex than they would seem from a superficial glance.

A liberation theology of the Americas that takes seriously on-the-
ground research must be hemispheric. Liberation theologians need to
stop speaking as a minority with localized interests and instead acknowledge that they are advocates for the majority of the world's population,
the global poor.[35] Even though the present academy has sidelined liberationist projects as advocacy theologies that address only a few, liberation
theologians should not accept this categorization of their work. However,
they should be open to non-Christian religions and renounce the Christian privilege that their theologies have historically embraced. Perhaps
they can learn from scholars who work in intercultural philosophy.[36]
Intercultural thought advocates a living together in the midst of difference. Diversity is seen as that which pushes us to change and grow.

Scholars of religion are united by the contested object of their study,
religion. The field suffers and benefits from what Ann Taves calls a "methodological promiscuity" that loosely binds us in ways that can facilitate
excellent interdisciplinary conversations.[37] The study of liberation theologies reveals that religion's interdisciplinary nature is our greatest gift
and is also our greatest challenge. This book does not join the chorus
of voices that claims the era of liberation theology is past and that we
should move on to other approaches within the field of theology. Yet
as a discipline that has historically prided itself on the clear categorization of religious traditions, identities, and practices, the study of religion
today is challenged by the multiple and hybrid ways in which religion
is practiced throughout the Americas. Instead of attempting to create

false constructs of insider/outsider, we need to embrace the religious hybridity that is our hemispheric landscape. This hybridity includes not only religious identity but also racial, ethnic, and national identities. We cannot allow academic categories to misrepresent the lived religion of the people themselves, whose everyday religious practices, struggles, and faith should be the focus of our research. Unless we study this concrete religion, our academic work risks fading into the oblivion of disengaged abstraction.

# NOTES

## NOTES FOR THE INTRODUCTION

1. In this book when I speak of the Americas I am referring to the Americas as a whole and not to the United States exclusively.
2. Although liberation theologians have increasingly examined the racial and ethnic diversity of the Americas, they have paid little attention to the religious diversity of the Americas.
3. D. G. Hart, *The University Gets Religion: Religious Studies in American Higher Education* (Baltimore, MD: Johns Hopkins University Press, 1999), 112.
4. Harold J. Recinos, "Introduction," in *Wading Through Many Voices: Toward a Theology of Public Conversation*, ed. Harold J. Recinos (Lanham, MD: Rowman & Littlefield, 2011), 3.
5. Margaret R. Miles, "Becoming Answerable for What We See," *Journal of the American Academy of Religion* 68:3 (2000): 471.
6. Ibid., 472.
7. Rebecca S. Chopp, "Beyond the Founding Fratricidal Conflict: A Tale of Three Cities," *Journal of the American Academy of Religion* 70:3 (2002): 467.
8. Elizabeth A. Johnson, *The Quest for the Living God: Mapping Frontiers in the Theology of God* (New York: Continuum, 2007), 73–74.
9. Miles, "Becoming Answerable," 472.
10. Chopp, "Beyond the Conflict," 463.
11. Stanley Fish, "Why We Built the Ivory Tower," *New York Times*, May 21, 2004.
12. Michael Eric Dyson, "Introduction: Why I Am an Intellectual," in *The Michael Eric Dyson Reader* (New York: Basic Civitas Books, 2004), ix.
13. Donald Wiebe, "An Eternal Return All Over Again: The Religious Conversation Endures," *Journal of the American Academy of Religion* 74:3 (2006): 674–696.
14. Donald Wiebe, *The Politics of Religious Studies* (New York: Palgrave Macmillan, 2000), xiii.

15. Robert A. Orsi, *Between Heaven and Earth: The Religious World People Make and the Scholars That Study Them* (Princeton, NJ: Princeton University Press, 2006), 151.

16. David D. Hall, "Introduction," in *Lived Religion in America: Toward a History of Practice*, ed. David D. Hall (Princeton, NJ: Princeton University Press, 1997), vii.

17. Meredith B. McGuire, *Lived Religion: Faith and Practice in Everyday Life* (New York: Oxford University Press, 2006), 12.

18. Robert A. Orsi, "Everyday Miracles: The Study of Lived Religion," in Hall, *Lived Religion in America*, 8.

19. Ibid., 9.

20. Sarah McFarland Taylor, *Green Sisters: A Spiritual Ecology* (Cambridge, MA: Harvard University Press, 2007), x.

21. Ibid., xii.

22. Ibid.

23. Thomas A. Tweed, *Our Lady of the Exile: Diasporic Religion at a Cuban Catholic Shrine in Miami* (New York: Oxford University Press, 1997), 10.

24. Nancy T. Ammerman, "Introduction: Observing Modern Religious Lives," in *Everyday Religion: Observing Modern Religious Lives*, ed. Nancy T. Ammerman (New York: Oxford University Press, 2007), 5.

25. "But this announcement of the demise of liberation theology is both parochial and questionable. With the violence, poverty, and oppression continuing and worsening in the world, the need for the liberating voice has not disappeared; rather liberation theology needs to be and has been restated for the new situation on a more global level." Rosemary Radford Ruether, "Catholicism," in *The Hope of Liberation in World Religions*, ed. Miguel A. De La Torre (Waco, TX: Baylor University Press, 2008), 19.

26. Joerg Rieger, *Christ and Empire: From Paul to Postcolonial Times* (Minneapolis: Fortress Press, 2007), 7.

27. Joerg Rieger, "Protestantism," in *The Hope of Liberation in World Religions*, ed. Miguel A. De La Torre (Waco, TX: Baylor University Press, 2008), 47.

28. "Western academia saw the popular theologian as a benevolent father dealing with ignorant, although sweet and well-disposed, native children. . . . Many Europeans would have liked to have submissive, faithful Christian natives in their parishes, instead of real people." Marcella María Althaus-Reid, "Gustavo Gutiérrez Goes to Disneyland: Theme Park Theologies and the Diaspora of the Discourse of the Popular Theologian in Liberation Theology," in *Interpreting Beyond Borders*, ed. Fernando F. Segovia (Sheffield, UK: Sheffield Academic Press, 2000), 37.

29. Ibid., 51–52.

30. Ibid., 42.

31. Barbara A. Holmes, *Race and the Cosmos* (Harrisburg, PA: Trinity Press International, 2002), 31.

32. "Liberation theology assumes that the common experience of oppression is sufficient to create the desire for a new coalition of dissident minorities." Vine Deloria, *For This Land: Writings on Religion in America* (New York: Routledge, 2000), 100.

33. Susan Brooks Thistlethwaite, "On Becoming a Traitor: The Academic Liberation Theologian and the Future," in *Liberating the Future: God, Mammon, and Theology*, ed. Joerg Rieger (Minneapolis: Fortress Press, 1998). 16.

34. In her introduction to *The Anthropology of Christianity*, Fenella Cannell highlights a similar trend in anthropology: Christianity serves as the obvious and therefore the repressed religion in the discipline. Christianity is the last major area of study explored by ethnographers. Fenella Cannell, "Introduction," in *The Anthropology of Christianity*, ed. Fenella Cannell (Durham, NC: Duke University Press, 2006), 1–50.

## NOTES FOR CHAPTER 1

1. In his overview of the method of liberation theologies throughout the globe, Vietnamese American theologian Peter Phan noted that this twentieth-century movement has been the most significant development in Christianity since the Reformation. Peter C. Phan, "Method in Liberation Theologies," *Theological Studies* 61 (2000): 40–63.

2. Leonardo and Clodovis Boff provide one of the most well-known and useful models for understanding the complexity of liberation theology as it saturates various levels of society. The Boff brothers outline three levels of liberation theology: the popular, the pastoral, and the academic. The popular is found in base communities; the pastoral is situated in pastoral institutes and study centers; the academic is in universities and seminaries. Leonardo Boff and Clodovis Boff, *Introducing Liberation Theology* (Maryknoll, NY: Orbis Books, 2001), 11–21.

3. As will be explored later in this section, I argue that *evangélico* movements are not exclusive to Protestantism but are also found in the growth of charismatic Catholicism in Latin America. I also specifically maintain the word *evangélico* in Spanish instead of translating it as "evangelical," for Anglo North American evangelical churches are quite different from their Latino/a and Latin American counterparts.

4. Daniel H. Levine, *Popular Voices in Latin American Catholicism* (Princeton, NJ: Princeton University Press, 1992), 10.

5. "As a practical matter, base communities range in emphasis from highly pietistic and devotional to socially activist, in structure from authoritarian to democratic, and in status from autonomous to utterly reliant on elites and institutions for guidance." Ibid., 13.

6. Leonardo Boff, *Ecclesiogenesis: The Base Communities Reinvent the Church* (Maryknoll, NY: Orbis Books, 1986), 2. For Boff it is important to maintain the apostolic validity of BCCs. As he writes, "*The church sprung from the people is the same as the church sprung from the apostles.*" Ibid., 7.

7. Ibid., 13. Boff, while commending Vatican II's emphasis on the local church, argues that it offered an incomplete understanding of the local church with its emphasis, in diocesan terms, of defining the local church in light of the Eucharist and the bishop. The 1968 conference of Latin American bishops in Medellín, in contrast, defined the local church from the "bottom up," acknowledging the church as a community of faith. The particular church is thus the universal Church concretized.

8. Leonardo Boff, *Church: Charism and Power: Liberation Theology and the Institutional Church* (New York: Crossroad, 1985), 10.

9. W. E. Hewitt, "For Defenders of the People to Defenders of the Faith: A 1984–1993 Retrospective of CEB Activity in São Paulo," *Latin American Perspectives* 25:1 (Jan. 1998): 174.

10. José Comblin, *Called for Freedom: The Changing Context of Liberation Theology* (Maryknoll, NY: Orbis Books, 1998), 14.

11. David Stoll, *Is Latin America Turning Protestant? The Politics of Evangelical Growth* (Berkeley: University of California Press, 1990), 3.

12. Although I agree that liberationist Catholicism tends to emphasize the structural, this is not the case for all Catholic liberationists, at both the pastoral and the academic levels. In other words, I find the evaluation to be a bit of an overstatement.

13. Edward L. Cleary, *The Rise of Charismatic Catholicism in Latin America* (Gainesville: University Press of Florida, 2011), 1.

14. Ibid., 61. In a similar vein, Marjo de Theije argues that the differences between CCR and Pentecostalism are not as extreme as often assumed. An interesting link between BCCs and Charismatic Catholicism is also seen in the work of Theije. Theije argues that CEBs and the CCR appear at first oppositional. BCCs emphasize a liberationist reading of Christianity and direct engagement in social action. The CCR movement emphasizes individual religious experience. But Theije believes that these two movements are not in fact antithetical. His work focuses on the Brazilian community of Garanhuns. Both are lay-led movements within the parish. He discovered a cross-section of participation in both groups. Ideologically he finds little distinction between the two or at least not as pronounced a distinction as scholars assume. Because liberationist ideology has saturated the ethos of the parish for two decades, it functions, at some level, even in the CCR, where it influences the adoption of charismatic prayer rituals. Also, both groups privilege the interpretation of Scripture in their gatherings. Marjo de Theije, "Charismatic Renewal and Base Communities: The Religious Participation of Women in a Brazilian Parish," in *More Than Opium: An Anthropological Approach to Latin American and Caribbean Pentecostal Practice*, ed. Barbara Boudewijnse, A. F. Droogers, and Frans Kamsteeg (Lanham, MD: Scarecrow Press, 1998), 225–248.

15. R. Andrew Chesnut, "A Preferential Option for the Spirit: The Catholic Charismatic Renewal in Latin America's New Religious Economy," *Latin American Politics and Society* 45:1 (Spring 2003): 67.

16. Anna L. Peterson and Manuel A. Vásquez, eds., *Latin American Religions: Histories and Documents in Context* (New York: New York University Press, 2008), 242.

17. Jean Daudelin and W. E. Hewitt, "Latin American Politics: Exit the Catholic Church?" in *Organized Religion in the Political Transformation of Latin American*, ed. Satya R. Pattnayak (Lanham, MD: University Press of America, 1995), 177–194.

18. Cleary, Edward L., *Crisis and Change: The Church in Latin America Today* (Maryknoll, NY: Orbis Books, 1985), 127.

19. An excellent contextual study of the diversity of Christianity among Peruvians and Salvadorans, both in their homelands and in the United States, is found in Anna L. Peterson, Manuel Vásquez, and Philip Williams, eds., *Christianity, Social Change, and Globalization in the Americas* (New Brunswick, NJ: Rutgers University Press, 2001).

20. Donald E. Miller and Tetsunao Yamamori, *Global Pentecostalism: The New Face of Christian Social Engagement* (Berkeley: University of California Press, 2007), 182.

21. Anna L. Peterson and Manuel A. Vásquez, "'Upwards, Never Down': The Catholic Charismatic Renewal in Transnational Perspective," in Peterson, Vásquez, and Williams, *Christianity, Social Change, and Globalization*, 198.

22. Anna L. Peterson, Manuel A. Vásquez, and Philip J. Williams, "Introduction: Christianity and Social Change in the Shadow of Globalization," in Peterson, Vásquez, and Williams, *Christianity, Social Change, and Globalization*, 5.

23. Christian Smith, *The Emergence of Liberation Theology: Radical Religion and Social Movement Theory* (Chicago: University of Chicago Press, 1991).

24. Gustavo Gutiérrez, *A Theology of Liberation: History, Politics, and Salvation*, 15th anniversary ed. (Maryknoll, NY: Orbis Books, 1988).

25. Milagros Peña, "Liberation Theology in Peru: An Analysis of the Role of Intellectuals in Social Movements," *Journal for the Scientific Study of Religion* 33:1 (1994): 34–45.

26. Gustavo Gutiérrez, *We Drink from Our Own Wells: The Spiritual Journey of People.* (Maryknoll, NY: Orbis Books, 2003).

27. Enrique Dussel, "The Political and Ecclesial Context of Liberation Theology in Latin America," in *The Emergent Gospel: Theology from the Underside of History*, ed. Sergio Torres and Virginia Fabella (Maryknoll, NY: Orbis Books, 1978), 175.

28. Elina Vuola, "Radical Eurocentrism: The Crisis and Death of Latin America Liberation Theology and Recipes for Its Improvement," in *Interpreting the Postmodern: Responses to "Radical Orthodoxy,"* ed. Rosemary Radford Ruether and Marion Grau (New York: T & T Clark, 2006), 58.

29. Ibid., 62.

30. Otto A. Maduro, "Once Again Liberating Theology? Towards a Latin American Liberation Theological Self-Criticism," in *Liberation Theology and Sexuality*, 2nd ed., ed. Marcella Althaus-Reid (London: SCM Press, 2009), 23.

31. "The decisive weapon in the hands of the Vatican against doctrinal 'deviations' and 'excessively political' pastoral agents is the nomination of conservative

bishops, known for their open hostility to liberation theology." Michael Löwy, *The War of Gods: Religion and Politics in Latin America* (New York: Verso, 1996), 131.

32. Petter Hebblewaite, "Liberation Theology and the Roman Catholic Church," in *The Cambridge Companion to Liberation Theology*, 2nd ed., ed. Christopher Rowland (New York: Cambridge University Press, 2007), 213.

33. In the background of this document is the infamous Boff case, in which Brazilian theologian Leonardo Boff was silenced because of some ecclesiological teachings in his book *Church: Charism and Power*. In this text Boff argues that the grassroots communities in Latin America represent a pneumatological ecclesiology that is the new face of the Church. This pneumatological ecclesiology is in contrast to the hierarchical ecclesiology of the clergy.

34. Rosini Gibellini, *The Liberation Theology Debate* (Maryknoll, NY: Orbis Books, 1987), 46.

35. Daniel M. Bell Jr., *Liberation Theology after the End of History: The Refusal to Cease Suffering* (New York: Routledge, 2001).

36. Paul E. Sigmund, *Liberation Theology at the Crossroads: Democracy or Revolution?* (New York: Oxford University Press, 1990), 182.

37. Ibid., 188–189.

38. See, for example, the 1981 encyclical *Laborem Exercens*.

39. David Stoll, *Tongues of Fire: The Explosion of Protestantism in Latin America* (Oxford, UK: Blackwell, 1990), 290.

40. "By the end of the 1980s liberation theology was already suffering serious weaknesses. Its social analysis was more open to question, its theology was under attack, its supporters in Latin America were being replaced and its roots in the popular Church were weaker. It was still a powerful influence within the Church and theology but it was much less well equipped to cope with the dramatic changes that lay ahead." David Tombs, "Latin American Liberation Theology Faces the Future," in *Faith in the Millennium*, ed. Michael Hayes (Sheffield, UK: Sheffield Academic Press, 2001), 52.

41. Dependency theory is the theory that the resources from poor, underdeveloped countries flow to wealthy countries and that this economic structure benefits the developed world at the expense of the underdeveloped world.

42. Tombs, "Latin American Liberation Theology," 56.

43. Ibid., 128. In a similar vein, Carmelo Alvarez argues that there was an overemphasis on the political dimension of liberation theology. "In the confusion they missed the point: Liberation Theology is a praxis of faith that provides a methodology by which Christians committed to justice and the liberation of many oppressions get involved in socio-political, cultural movements and political parties in order to create the conditions toward a 'new society' more just, fraternal, and equal." Carmelo E. Alvarez, "Is Liberation Theology Finished?" *Encounter* 59:1–2 (1998): 203.

44. Jennifer S. Hughes, "The Catholic Church and Social Revolutionaries," in *Religion and Society in Latin America: Interpretive Essays from Conquest to Present*, ed. Lee M. Penyal and Walter J. Petry (Maryknoll, NY: Orbis Books, 2009), 263.

45. Gutiérrez, *We Drink*; Gustavo Gutiérrez, *On Job: God-Talk and the Suffering of the Innocent* (Maryknoll, NY: Orbis Books, 1999)

46. See Rubem A. Alves, *The Poet, the Warrior, the Prophet* (London: SCM Press; Philadelphia: Trinity Press International, 1990), and Rubem A. Alves, "From Liberation Theologian to Poet: A Plea That the Church Move from Ethics to Aesthetics, from Doing to Beauty," *Church and State* 83 (1993): 20–24. Marcella María Althaus-Reid, *Indecent Theology: Theological Perversions in Sex, Gender and Politics* (London and New York: Routledge, 2000), and Marcella María Althaus-Reid, "Gustavo Gutiérrez Goes to Disneyland: Theme Park Theologies and the Diaspora of the Discourse of the Popular Theologian in Liberation Theology," in Fernando F. Segovia, ed., *Interpreting Beyond Borders* (Sheffield, UK: Sheffield Academic Press, 2000), 36–58.

47. Sigmund, *Liberation Theology at the Crossroads*, 177. Sigmund's full analysis carries through page 188 of the text.

48. CELAM, "Medellín Conclusiones: La Iglesia en la actual transformación de América Latina a la Luz del Concilio," in *Segunda conferencia general del Episcopado Latinoamericano*, ed. Episcopado Latinoamericano (Medellín, Colombia: Consejo Episcopal Latino Americano, 1968), 68.

49. Michael R. Candelaria, *Popular Religion and Liberation: The Dilemma of Liberation Theology* (Albany: State University Press of New York, 1990). For another overview of different views on popular religion in Latin America, see Thomas A. Kselman, "Ambivalence and Assumption in the Concept of Popular Religion," in *Religion and Political Conflict in Latin America*, ed. Daniel H. Levine (Chapel Hill: University of North Carolina Press, 1986), 24–41, and Tokihiro Kudó, *Práctica religiosa y proyecto histórico: Estudio sobre la religiosidad popular en dos barrios en Lima*. Lima, Peru: CEP, 1980.

50. Candelaria, *Popular Religion and Liberation*, 9.

51. Ibid., 118.

52. An excellent example of such writing is *Popular Religion*. This book, published by the theological review *Concilium* in 1986, has articles by Rosemary Radford Ruether, Virgilio Elizondo, and Leonardo Boff; it examines popular religion in Europe, the United States, and Latin America. Norbert Greinacher and Norbert Mette, eds., *Popular Religion* (Edinburgh: T & T Clark, 1986).

53. Jennifer Scheper Hughes, *Biography of a Mexican Crucifix: Lived Religion and Local Faith from the Conquest to the Present* (New York: Oxford University Press, 2010), 242.

54. Ibid., 15.

55. María Pilar Aquino, *Our Cry for Life: Feminist Theology from Latin America* (Maryknoll, NY: Orbis Books, 1993).

56. Ibid., 179.
57. Henry Goldschmidt and Elizabeth McAlister, eds., *Race, Nation, and Religion in the Americas* (New York: Oxford University Press, 2004).
58. "The popular/lived religion model has been utilized most often by anthropologists and religious studies scholars, while church and state approaches have been adopted primarily by political scientists and historians. Another theoretical perspective that has gained increasing favor among a number of social scientists studying religion in Latin America (and elsewhere) is the 'rational choice' paradigm and its associated 'religious market' approach, which draw from models first developed in the field of economics and then adapted to sociology and political science." Anna L. Peterson and Manuel A. Vásquez, "Introduction," in Peterson and Vásquez, *Latin American Religions*, 14.
59. Althaus-Reid, *Indecent Theology*.
60. Marcella María Althaus-Reid, "Class, Sex, and the Theologian: Reflections on the Liberationist Movement in Latin America," in *Another Possible World: Reclaiming Liberation Theology*, ed. Marcella María Althaus-Reid, Ivan Petrella, and Luis Carlos Susin (London: SCM Press, 2007), 28–29.
61. Marcella María Althaus-Reid, "Demythologizing Liberation Theology: Reflections on Power, Poverty, and Sexuality," in *The Cambridge Companion to Liberation Theology*, 2nd ed., ed. Christopher Rowland (New York: Cambridge University Press, 2007), 127.
62. Althaus-Reid's concerns are echoed in Mark Lewis Taylor's scholarship on the entitled advocates of subalterns in liberation theology. "The program of the benevolent western intellectual has regularly been to identify and then to assimilate Third World people as others, making a place for them, believing this to be the doing of good." Yet this project can be a form of imperialism, for the scholar controls the voice of the marginalized. Mark Lewis Taylor, "Subalternity and Advocacy as *Kairos* for Theology," in *Opting for the Margins: Postmodernity and Liberation in Christian Theology*, ed. Joerg Rieger (New York: Oxford University Press, 2003), 32
63. Ibid., 34–40.
64. Frank Graziano, *Cultures of Devotion: Folk Saints of Spanish America* (New York: Oxford University Press, 2007).
65. As Asian feminist theologian Kwok Pui Lan emphasizes, "When we consider the diversity of the poor and oppressed in the world, we must reckon with the fact that the majority of them are non-Christians." Kwok Pui Lan, "Liberation Theology in the Twenty-First Century," in Rieger, *Opting for the Margins*, 77.
66. Aloysius Pieris, *An Asian Theology of Liberation* (Edinburgh: T & T Clark, 1988), 87.
67. Elizabeth A. Johnson, *The Quest for the Living God: Mapping Frontiers in the Theology of God* (New York: Continuum, 2007), 74.

68. Gustavo Gutiérrez, "Renewing the Option for the Poor," in *Liberation Theologies, Postmodernity, and the Americas*, ed. David Batstone, Eduardo Mendieta, Lois Ann Lorentzen, and Dwight N. Hopkins (New York: Routledge, 1991), 72.

69. Franz J. Hinkelammert, "Liberation Theology in the Economic and Social Context of Latin America: Economy and Theology, or the Irrationality of the Rationalized," in Batstone, Mendieta, Lorentzen, and Hopkins, *Liberation Theologies, Postmodernity*, 27.

70. "Throughout his writings, Gutiérrez is quite clear that the warrants for a preferential option for the poor are, above all, *theocentric*." Roberto S. Goizueta, "Knowing the God of the Poor: The Preferential Option for the Poor," in Rieger, *Opting for the Margins*, 145. Although Gutiérrez's early work tends to emphasize the continuity between human liberative action and God's liberation in history, in his book on Job he emphasizes the discontinuity. "Gutiérrez's reflection on Job also opens new avenues in liberation theology due to its stress on the discontinuity between human agency and God's agency. God's action and God's reasons for acting cannot be simply subsumed to the way humans act and reason." Gaspar Martinez, *Confronting the Mystery of God: Political, Liberation, and Public Theologies* (New York: Continuum, 2001, 149).

71. Pablo Richard, "Theology in the Theology of Liberation," in *Mysterium Liberationis: Fundamental Concepts of Liberation Theology*, ed. Ignacio Ellacuría and Jon Sobrino (Maryknoll, NY: Orbis Books, 1993), 52.

72. Althaus-Reid, *Indecent Theology*, 31.

NOTES FOR CHAPTER 2

1. Anthony B. Pinn, "Black Theology," in *Liberation Theologies in the United States: An Introduction*, ed. Stacey M. Floyd Thomas and Anthony B. Pinn (New York: New York University Press, 2010), 17.

2. National Committee of Negro Churchmen, "Black Power," reprinted in *Black Theology: A Documentary History*, vol. 1, *1966–1979*, ed. James H. Cone and Gayraud S. Wilmore (Maryknoll, NY: Orbis Books, 1993), 19–26; James H. Cone, *Black Theology and Black Power* (Maryknoll, NY: Orbis Books, 1997).

3. "Womanist 1. From *womanish*. (Opp. of 'girlish,' i.e. frivolous, irresponsible, not serious.) A black feminist or feminist of color." Alice Walker, "Definition of a Womanist," in *In Search of Our Mother's Gardens: Womanist Prose* (San Francisco: Harcourt Brace, 1983), xi.

4. Karen Baker-Fletcher, "Passing on the Spark: A Womanist Perspective on Theology and Culture," in *Changing Conversations: Religious Reflection and Cultural Analysis*, ed. Dwight N. Hopkins and Sheila Greeve Davaney (New York: Routledge, 1996), 149.

5. James H. Cone, *God of the Oppressed* (San Francisco: Harper San Francisco, 1975), 136.

6. Dennis W. Wiley, "God," in *The Cambridge Companion to Black Theology*, ed. Dwight N. Hopkins and Edward P. Antonio (New York: Cambridge University Press, 2012), 87.

7. M. Shawn Copeland, "Poor Is the Color of God," in *The Option for the Poor in Christian Theology*, ed. Daniel G. Groody (Notre Dame, IN: University of Notre Dame Press, 2007), 226.

8. For an overview of black liberation theology, see Dwight N. Hopkins, *Black Theology of Liberation* (Maryknoll, NY: Orbis Books), 1999.

9. Anthony B. Pinn, *Terror and Triumph: The Nature of Black Religion* (Minneapolis: Fortress Press, 2003); Victor Anderson, *Creative Exchange: A Constructive Theology of African American Religious Experience* (Minneapolis: Fortress Press, 2009).

10. Pinn, "Black Theology," 32.

11. Anderson, *Creative Exchange*.

12. Marla F. Frederick, *Between Sundays: Black Women and Everyday Struggles of Faith* (Berkeley: University of California Press, 2003).

13. For a description of this project, see Dwight N. Hopkins and George C.L. Cummings, eds., *Cut Loose Your Stammering Tongue: Black Theology in the Slave Narrative*, 2nd ed. (Louisville, KY: Westminster John Knox Press, 2003).

14. Victor Anderson, *Beyond Ontological Blackness: An Essay on African American Religious and Cultural Criticism* (New York: Continuum, 1995), 98.

15. Diana L. Hayes, "To Be the Bridge: Voices from the Margins," in *A Dream Unfinished: Theological Reflections on America from the Margins*, ed. Eleazar S. Fernandez and Fernando F. Segovia (Maryknoll, NY: Orbis Books, 2001), 52–71.

16. Marcia Y. Riggs, "'What Happens to a Dream Deferred?' Reflections and Hopes of a Member of a Transitional Generation," in Fernandez and Segovia, *A Dream Unfinished*, 88–97.

17. Marcia Y. Riggs, "Escaping the Polarity of Race versus Gender and Ethnicity," in *Wading Through Many Voices: Toward a Theology of Public Conversation*, ed. Harold J. Recinos (Lanham, MD: Rowman and Littlefield, 2011), 39.

18. Anthony B. Pinn, *Varieties of African American Religious Experience* (Minneapolis: Fortress Press, 1998), 194.

19. Anthea D. Butler, *Women in the Church of God in Christ: Making a Sanctified World* (Chapel Hill: University of North Carolina Press, 2007), 2.

20. Pinn, "Black Theology," 25.

21. Stephanie Mitchem, *African American Folk Healing* (New York: New York University Press, 2007), 4.

22. Butler, *Women*, 10.

23. Charles H. Long, "Assessment and New Departures for a Study of Black Religion in the United States of America," in *African American Religious Thought: An Anthology*, ed. Cornel West and Eddie S. Glaude Jr. (Louisville, KY: Westminster John Knox Press, 2003), 221–235.

24. William R. Jones, *Is God a White Racist? A Preamble to Black Theology* (Boston: Beacon Press, 1997).

25. James H. Cone, *The Cross and the Lynching Tree* (Maryknoll, NY: Orbis Books, 2011), 124.

26. See Michelle A. Gonzalez, *Afro-Cuban Theology: Religion, Race, Culture, and Identity* (Gainesville: University Press of Florida, 2006).

27. See Cheryl J. Sanders, "Christian Ethics and Theology in Womanist Perspective," in Cone and Wilmore, *Black Theology*, vol. 2, *1980–1992*, 336–344; Anderson, *Beyond Ontological Blackness*.

28. Bryan N. Massingale, *Racial Justice and the Catholic Church* (Maryknoll, NY: Orbis Books, 2010). See also Willie J. Jenning, *The Christian Imagination: Theology and the Origins of Race* (New Haven, CT: Yale University Press, 2010).

29. West and Glaude, *African American Religious Thought*.

30. Cornel West and Eddie S. Glaude Jr., "Introduction: Towards New Visions and New Approaches in African American Religious Studies," in ibid., xii. It is interesting to note that an earlier book on African American religious thought focused on Christian theology exclusively. Gayraud S. Wilmore, ed., *African American Religious Studies: An Interdisciplinary Anthology"* (Durham: Duke University Press, 1989).

31. James H. Evans, "The Future of Black Theology," in Hopkins and Antonio, *Cambridge Companion to Black Theology*, 313.

32. Gayraud S. Wilmore, "Black Theology at the Turn of the Century: Some Unmet Needs and Challenges," in *Black Faith and Public Talk: Critical Essays on James H. Cone's "Black Theology and Black Power,"* ed. Dwight N. Hopkins (Maryknoll, NY: Orbis Books, 1999), 239.

33. Cornel West, "The Crisis in Contemporary American Religion," in *The Cornel West Reader* (New York: Civitas Books, 1999), 357–359.

34. Cornel West, "Christian Theological Mediocrity," in *Prophetic Fragments* (Grand Rapids, MI: Eerdman, 1988), 195–196.

35. West, "The Crisis in Theological Education," in West, *Prophetic Fragments*, 273.

36. Wilmore, "Black Theology at the Turn of the Century," 238.

37. Barbara Dianne Savage, *Your Spirits Walk Beside Us: The Politics of Black Religion* (Cambridge, MA: Harvard University Press, 2008), 9. Savage offers an excellent study of black Christianity in the twentieth century. She challenges the assumption that black churches have been a site of political activism throughout the twentieth century.

38. J. Kameron Carter, *Race: A Theological Account* (New York, NY: Oxford University Press, 2008).

39. Monica Coleman, *Making a Way Out of No Way: A Womanist Theology* (Minneapolis: Fortress Press, 2008).

40. Pinn, "Black Theology," 25.

41. Jwanza Eric Clark, *Indigenous Black Theology: Toward an African-Centered Theology of the African-American Religious Experience* (Gordonsville, PA: Palgrave Macmillan, 2012), 2–3.

42. Cone, *The Cross and the Lynching Tree*, xiv–xv.

43. M. Shawn Copeland, *Enfleshing Freedom: Body, Race, and Being* (Minneapolis: Fortress Press, 2010), 7.

44. Anthony B. Pinn, *What Is African American Religion?* (Minneapolis: Fortress Press, 2011), 22.

45. Butler, *Women*.

46. Jones, *Is God a White Racist?*; Pinn, *Why Lord? Suffering and Evil in Black Theology* (New York: Continuum, 1995); Delores S. Williams, *Sisters in the Wilderness: The Challenge of Womanist God-Talk* (Maryknoll, NY: Orbis Books, 1993).

47. Pinn, *Why Lord?*, 157.

NOTES FOR CHAPTER 3

1. Orlando O. Espín and Miguel H. Díaz, "Introduction," in *From the Heart of Our People: Latino/a Explorations in Systematic Theology*, ed. by Orlando O. Espín and Miguel H. Díaz (Maryknoll, NY: Orbis Books, 1999), 2–3.

2. Nancy Pineda-Madrid, "Latina Theology," in *Liberation Theologies in the United States*, ed. Stacey M. Floyd Thomas and Anthony B. Pinn (New York: New York University Press, 2010), 69.

3. Loida Martell-Ortero, "Women Doing Theology: Una Perspectiva Evangélica," *Apuntes* 14 (1994): 67–85. In a groundbreaking textbook, Isasi-Díaz elaborates an early definition of *mujerista*. "A *mujerista* is a Hispanic woman who struggles to liberate herself not as an individual but as a member of a Hispanic community. . . . A *mujerista* is a Latina who makes a preferential option for herself and her Hispanic sisters, understanding that our struggle for liberation has to take into consideration how racism/ethnic prejudice, economic oppression, and sexism work together and reinforce each other." Ada María Isasi-Díaz, *En la Lucha / In the Struggle: Elaborating a Mujerista Theology* (Minneapolis: Fortress Press, 1993), 4.

4. Eduardo C. Fernández, *Mexican-American Catholics* (New York: Paulist Press, 2007), 90. Fernández's introduction to Latino/a theology, *La Cosecha: Harvesting Contemporary United States Hispanic Theology (1972–1998)* (Collegeville, MN: Liturgical Press, 2000), is dedicated to introducing Latino/a theology as a contextual theology.

5. Miguel A. De La Torre and Edwin David Aponte, *Introducing Latino/a Theologies* (Maryknoll, NY: Orbis Books, 2001), 43.

6. Ibid., 72.

7. Benjamín Valentín, "Hispanic/Latino(a) Theology," in Floyd Thomas and Pinn, *Liberation Theologies in the United States*, 103.

8. Fernando F. Segovia, "Toward Latino/a American Biblical Criticism: Latino(a) ness as Problematic," in *They Were All Together in One Place? Toward Minority Biblical Criticism*, ed. Randall C. Bailey, Tat-Siong Benny Liew, and Fernando F. Segovia (Atlanta: Society of Biblical Literature, 2009), 193–226.

9. "The task of theology remains abundantly clear: theology serves the church by informing and correcting its proclamation of the Word of God in an ever-changing world." Ruben Rosario Rodríguez, *Racism and God-Talk: A Latino/a Perspective* (New York: New York University Press, 2008), 8.

10. Timothy M. Matovina, ed., *Beyond Borders: Writings of Virgilio Elizondo and Friends* (Maryknoll, NY: Orbis Books, 2000).

11. Virgilio Elizondo, "*Mestizaje* as a Locus for Theological Reflection," in *Frontiers of Hispanic Theology*, ed. Allan Figueroa Deck (Maryknoll, NY: Orbis Books, 1992), 106.

12. Espín and Díaz, "Introduction," in Espín and Díaz, *From the Heart of Our People*, 1.

13. A similar methodological gesture is found in the anthology *In Our Own Voices: Latino/a Renditions of Theology*. This book, to which I am a contributor, offers a constructive reading of classic doctrines in Christian theology from a Latino/a perspective. In his introduction to the book, editor Benjamín Valentín argues that "it is reasonable to claim that the effort to interpret, to evaluate, and to reformulate the meanings of themes or doctrines such as God, Creation, human nature, human sin, Christ, the church, and eschatology, for instance, has received sparse consideration in the works of Latino/a theologians." Benjamín Valentín, "Introduction," in *In Our Own Voices: Latino/a Renditions of Theology*, ed. Benjamín Valentín (Maryknoll, NY: Orbis Books, 2010), xii.

14. Harold J. Recinos, "Introduction," in *Jesus in the Hispanic Community: Images of Christ from Theology to Popular Religion*, ed. Harold J. Recinos and Hugo Magallanes (Louisville, KY: Westminster John Knox Press, 2009), xiii.

15. Edwin David Aponte, "Metaphysical Blending in Latino/a Botánicas in Dallas," in *Rethinking Latino(a) Religion and Identity*, ed. Miguel A. De La Torres and Gastón Espinosa (Cleveland, OH: Pilgrim Press, 2006), 58.

16. Edwin David Aponte, *¡Santo! Varieties of Latino/a Spirituality* (Maryknoll, NY: Orbis Books, 2012).

17. "Hispanic theology is *of the struggling and suffering poor* and a theology *for the poor* and all others willing to listen to its insights. . . . [A] Hispanic theology emerges from the margins and speaks on behalf of those on the periphery to those at the centers of power." Samuel Solivan, "Sources of Hispanic / Latino American Theology: A Pentecostal Perspective," in *Hispanic/Latino Theology: Challenge and Promise*, ed. Ada María Isasi-Díaz and Fernando F. Segovia (Minneapolis: Fortress Press, 1996), 137.

18. De La Torre and Aponte, *Introducing Latino/a Theologies*, 53.

19. Michael E. Lee, "A Way Forward for Latino/a Christology," in Valentín, *In Our Own Voices*, 124.

20. "By which criteria, and grounded how, have we claimed all those things for the 'people' and for whatever might be 'popular'?" The word *popular* was most likely borrowed from Latin American liberation theology. Orlando O. Espín, "The State of U.S. Latino/a Theology," in *Hispanic Christian Thought at the Dawn of the 21st Century: Apuntes in Honor of Justo L. González*, ed. Alvin Padilla, Roberto Goizueta, and Edwin Villafañe (Nashville, TN: Abingdon Press, 2005), 102.

21. David Traverzo Galerzo, "Evangélicos," in Miguel A. De La Torre and Edwin David Aponte, *Handbook of Latino/a Theologies* (St. Louis, MO: Chalice Press, 2006), 194.

22. See Orlando O. Espín, ed., *Building Bridges, Doing Justice: Constructing a Latino/a Ecumenical Theology* (Maryknoll, NY: Orbis Books, 2009). The chapters in the book are papers from the 2008 ACHTUS meeting, which invited Protestant Latino/a theologians to an ecumenical dialogue.

23. Lee, "A Way Forward," 112.

24. Arlene M. Sánchez Walsh, "Pentecostals," in De La Torre and Aponte, *Handbook of Latino/a Theologies*, 199.

25. Gastón Espinosa, "History and Theory in the Study of Mexican-American Religions," in *Mexican American Religions: Spirituality, Activism, and Culture*, ed. Gastón Espinosa and Mario T. García (Durham, NC: Duke University Press, 2008), 37

26. Ibid., 70.

27. Gastón Espinosa, Virgilio Elizondo, and Jesse Miranda, eds. *Latino Religions and Civic Activism in the United States* (New York: Oxford University Press, 2005).

28. Luis D. León, *La Llorona's Children: Religion, Life, and Death in the U.S.-Mexican Borderlands* (Berkeley: University of California Press, 2004).

29. David Badillo, *Latino/as and the New Immigrant Church* (Baltimore: Johns Hopkins University Press, 2006).

30. Timothy M. Matovina, *Guadalupe and Her Faithful: Latino Catholics in San Antonio, from Colonial Origins to the Present* (Baltimore: Johns Hopkins University Press, 2005). Matovina's more recent book on Latino/a Catholicism applies the same methodology to the broader Latino/a Roman Catholic community: *Latino Catholicism: Transformation in America's Largest Church* (Princeton, NJ: Princeton University Press, 2011).

31. Thomas A. Tweed, *Our Lady of Exile: Diasporic Religion at a Cuban Catholic Shrine in Miami* (New York: Oxford University Press, 1997). A similar study of the Holy Child of Atocha is found in Juan Javier Pescador, *Crossing Borders with the Santo Niño de Atocha* (Albuquerque: University of New Mexico Press, 2009).

32. Kristy Nabhan-Warren, *The Virgin of El Barrio: Marian Apparitions, Catholic Evangelizing, and Mexican American Activism* (New York: New York University Press, 2005), 3.

33. Anthony M. Stevens-Arroyo and Ana María Diaz-Stevens, eds., *An Enduring Flame: Studies on Latino Popular Religiosity* (New York: Program for the Analysis of Religion among Latinos, 1994); Anthony M. Stevens-Arroyo and Gilbert R. Cadena, eds., *Old Masks, New Faces: Religion and Latino Identities* (New York: Program for the Analysis of Religion among Latinos, 1995); Anthony M. Stevens-Arroyo and Andrés Pérez y Mena, eds., *Enigmatic Powers: Syncretism with African and Indigenous Peoples' Religions among Latinos* (New York: Program for the Analysis of Religion among Latinos, 1995); Anthony M. Stevens-Arroyo and Segundo Pantoja, eds., *Discovering Latino Religion: A Comprehensive Social Science Bibliography* (New York: Program for the Analysis of Religion among Latinos, 1995).

34. Gastón Espinosa, "Methodological Reflections on Social Science Research on Latino Religions," in De La Torre and Espinosa, *Rethinking Latino(a) Religion*, 42.

35. "Although people who belong to the institutional church engage in popular religious practices, they, through these same practices, offer a critique of the institution. In that sense we can say that liberation theology is a form of popular religion." James Emprereur and Eduardo S. Fernández, *La Vida Sacra: Contemporary Hispanic Sacramental Theology* (Lanham, MD: Rowman and Littlefield, 2006), 5.

36. See Roberto S. Goizueta, "U.S. Hispanic Popular Catholicism as Theopoetics," in Isasi-Díaz and Segovia, *Hispanic / Latino Theology*, 268. In his discussion of Latino/a popular religion as the religion of the marginalized and as that which is most "ours," he relies heavily on Orlando O. Espín and Sixto García, "'Lilies of the Field': A Hispanic Theology of Providence and Human Responsibility," *Proceedings of the Catholic Theological Society of America* 44 (1989): 73.

37. De La Torre and Aponte, *Introducing Latino/a Theologies*, 118–119.

38. Orlando O. Espín, "Popular Catholicism among Latinos," in *Hispanic Catholic Culture in the U.S.: Issues and Concerns*, ed. Jay P. Dolan and Alan Figueroa Deck (Notre Dame, IN: University of Notre Dame Press, 1994), 308.

39. Ibid., 310.

40. Espín, "Traditioning: Culture, Daily Life, and Popular Religion, and Their Impact on the Christian Tradition," in *Futuring Our Past: Explorations in the Theology of Tradition*, ed. Orlando O. Espín and Gary Macy (Maryknoll, NY: Orbis Books, 2006), 9.

41. Ibid., 50.

42. Espín, "*Pasión y respeto:* Elizondo's Contribution to the Study of Popular Catholicism," in *Beyond Borders: Writings of Virgilio Elizondo and Friends*, ed. Timothy M. Matovina (Maryknoll, NY: Orbis Books, 2000), 102.

43. Virgilio Elizondo, "Popular Religion as Support of Identity," in Matovina, *Beyond Borders*, 126.

44. "Popular religion, within the frame of these normative hierarchies, is the experience of dark, poor, alien folk, or children and women, of the colonized, enslaved, and 'primitive,' of the ignorant or uneducated." Robert A. Orsi, *The Madonna of*

*115th Street: Faith and Community in Italian Harlem, 1880–1950*, 2nd ed. (New Haven, CT: Yale University Press, 2002), xiv.

45. Ibid., xvi.
46. Ibid., xix.
47. Meredith B. McGuire, *Lived Religion: Faith and Practice in Everyday Life* (New York: Oxford University Press, 2008), 47.
48. Anna L. Peterson and Manuel A. Vásquez, "Introduction," in *Latin American Religions: Histories and Documents in Context*, ed. Anna L. Peterson and Manuel A. Vásquez (New York: New York University Press, 2008), 7
49. Jorge A. Aquino, "The Prophetic Horizon of Latino Theology," in De La Torre and Espinosa, *Rethinking Latino(a) Religion*, 103.
50. Timothy M. Matovina and Gary Riebe-Estrella, eds., *Horizons of the Sacred: Mexican Traditions in U.S. Catholicism* (Ithaca, NY: Cornell University Press, 2002).
51. Nabhan-Warren, *The Virgin of El Barrio*, 217.
52. Arlene M. Sánchez Walsh, "Christology from a Latino/a Perspective: Pentecostalism," in Recinos and Magallanes, *Jesus in the Hispanic Community*, 96.
53. "A theological aesthetics grounded in U.S. Latino/a popular Catholicism reflects the intrinsic connection between worship, social justice, and theological truth." Roberto S. Goizueta, *Christ Our Companion: Toward a Theological Aesthetics of Liberation* (Maryknoll, NY: Orbis Books, 2009), 126.
54. See Manuel J. Mejido, "A Critique of the 'Aesthetic Turn' in U.S. Hispanic Theology: A Dialogue with Roberto Goizueta and the Positing of a New Paradigm," *Journal of Hispanic Latino Theology* 8:3 (Feb. 2001): 18–48.
55. This claim goes contrary to the claim by Mejido, who sees the "aesthetic turn" in Latino/a theology as alienating theology from the everyday struggles of Latino/a communities. Ibid.

NOTES FOR CHAPTER 4

1. Dianne M. Stewart, "Dancing Limbo: Black Passages through the Boundaries of Place, Race, Class, and Religion," in *Deeper Shades of Purple: Womanism in Religion and Society*, ed. Stacey M. Floyd-Thomas (New York: New York University Press, 2006), 93.
2. Dianne M. Stewart, "Womanist God-Talk on the Cutting Edge of Theology and Black Religious Studies: Assessing the Contribution of Delores Williams," in *Union Seminary Quarterly Review*, 58:3–4 (Fall 2004), 8, citing Delores Williams, *Sisters in the Wilderness: The Challenge of Womanist God-Talk* (Maryknoll, NY: Orbis Books, 1993).
3. Robert Warrior, "Canaanites, Cowboys, and Indians," in *Natives and Christians*, ed. James Treat (New York: Routledge, 1996), 93–104.
4. Edward P. Antonio, *Inculturation and Postcolonial Discourse in African Theology* (New York: Peter Lang, 2006); Emmanuel Martey, *African Theology: Inculturation and Liberation* (Maryknoll, NY: Orbis Books, 1995).

5. Maricel Mena López, "Globalization and Gender Inequality: A Contribution from a Latino Afro-Feminist Perspective," in *The Oxford Handbook of Feminist Theology*, ed. Mary McClintock Fulkerson and Sheila Briggs (New York: Oxford University Press, 2012), 168.

6. The debate over the way in which Catholicism has shaped or influenced Santería religion continues. Even though it is no longer required, Santería practitioners are often baptized. They also use the Catholic calendar of saints' days and make the required visit to a church immediately after initiation. "It would be futile to negate the extreme importance of the presence of Catholicism as an influential factor in the process of adaptation for the Africans. It would be just as futile to pretend that this encounter has not taken its toll on elements of Yoruba religion that as a result may have been modified or diluted. Yet, had Catholicism not been the dominant religious form, I speculate that African religions in the New World would not have survived intact." Miguel "Willie" Ramos, "Afro-Cuban Orisha Worship," in *Santería Aesthetics in Contemporary Latin American Art*, ed. Arturo Lindsay (Washington, DC: Smithsonian Institution Press, 1996), 55.

7. Elizabeth McAlister, "From Slave Revolt to a Blood Pact with Satan: The Evangelical Rewriting of Haitian History," *Studies in Religion* 41:2 (2012): 190.

8. Kate Ramsey, "Legislating 'Civilization' in Postrevolutionary Haiti," in *Race, Nation, and Religion in the Americas*, ed. Henry Goldschmidt and Elizabeth MacAlister (New York: Oxford University Press, 2004), 237.

9. Karen McCarthy Brown, "Staying Grounded in a High-Rise Building: Ecological Dissonance and Ritual Accommodation in Haitian Vodou," in *Gods of the City: Religion and the American Urban Landscape*, ed. Robert A. Orsi (Bloomington: Indiana University Press, 1999), 94.

10. Laënnec Hurbon, "Globalization and the Evolution of Haitian Vodou," in *Òrìṣà Devotion as World Religion: The Globalization of Yorùbá Religious Culture*, ed. Jacob K. Olupona and Terry Rey (Madison: University of Wisconsin Press, 2008), 274.

11. Dianne M. Stewart, "Orisha Traditions in the West," in *The Hope of Liberation in World Religions*, ed. Miguel A. De La Torre (Waco, TX: Baylor University Press, 2008), 240.

12. For a study of Yoruba identity among African Americans in the mid-twentieth century, see Tracey E. Hucks, "From Cuban Santería to African Yorùbá: Evolutions in African American Òrìṣà History, 1959–1970," in Olupona and Rey, *Òrìṣà Devotion as World Religion*, 337–354.

13. "Attempts by Owu, the primary force in southern Yorubaland, to suppress the kidnapping of Oyo slave traders by Ijebu raiders provoked a wide-scale conflict with the Ijebu. With the aid of displaced refugees from the Oyo civil wars, Owu was destroyed by 1821. . . . After a series of successful attacks from Dahomey, internal warfare, and Muslim rebellion in the first third of the nineteenth century, the Oyo Empire collapsed completely." Michele Reid, "The Yoruba in Cuba: Origins,

Identities, and Transformations," in *The Yoruba Diaspora in the Atlantic World*, ed. Toyin Falola and Matt D. Childs (Bloomington: Indiana University Press, 2004), 114.

14. The origins of the name *Lucumí* remain unclear. A French map from the eighteenth century shows a region labeled "Ulcumi" near Benin. Another, undated, map shows the kingdom of Oulcoumi in Yorubaland. Isabel Castellanos, "From Ulkumí to Lucumí: A Historical Overview of Religious Acculturation in Cuba," in *Santería Aesthetics*, 39–41. In addition to acknowledging the possibility that Lucumí comes from the Yoruba kingdom known as Ulkama or Ulkami, scholars also speculate that the origins of the term may be the Yoruba common greeting "oloku mí." Reid, "The Yoruba in Cuba," 115.

15. Mercedes Cros Sandoval, *Worldview, the Orichas, and Santería: Africa to Cuba and Beyond* (Gainesville: University of Florida Press, 2006), 48.

16. Citing the work of E. Bolaji Idowu, Ramos describes the term *orisha* as a corruption of the word *orishe*. *Ori* means head or source and *she* means to begin. "The name *orisha* would then be an ellipsis of *ibiti ori ti she*—the origin or source of *ori*: Olodumare himself." Ramos, "Afro-Cuban Orisha Worship," 56.

17. Ibid., 59.

18. Stewart, "Orisha Traditions in the West," 240–241.

19. Daniel H. Brown, "Altared Spaces: Afro-Cuban Religions and the Urban Landscape in Cuba and the United Sates," in Orsi, *Gods of the City*, 160.

20. "In broader Afro-Cuban religious cosmology, spirits are often thought to be crucial components of a person's own spiritual constitution, of his or her own *personhood,* simultaneously independent as protective agents and fundamentally related to those they protect." Diana Espirito Santo, "The Power of the Dead: Spirits, Socialism, and Selves in an Afro-Cuban Universe," *Fieldwork in Religion* 3:2 (2008), 163.

21. See Jacob K. Olupona and Regina Gemignani, *African Immigrant Religions in America* (New York: New York University Press, 2007); Kristina Witrz, *Ritual, Discourse, and Community in Cuban Santería* (Gainesville: University Press of Florida, 2007); Kamari Maxine Clarke, *Mapping Yorùbá Networks: Power and Agency in the Making of Transnational Communities* (Durham, NC: Duke University Press, 2004); Margarite Fernández Olmos and Lizabeth Paravisini-Gebert, eds., *Sacred Possessions: Vodou, Santería, Obeah and the Caribbean* (New Brunswick, NJ: Rutgers University Press, 2007).

22. Joseph M. Murphy, *Santería: African Spirits in America* (Boston: Beacon Press, 1993), xv.

23. Another excellent example of the participant-observer method is Todd Ramón Ochoa's *Society of the Dead: Quita Manaquita and Palo Praise in Cuba* (Berkeley: University of California Press, 2010).

24. Karen McCarthy Brown, *Mama Lola: A Vodou Priestess in Brooklyn* (Berkeley: University of California Press, 1991).

25. Carolyn Morrow Long, *Spiritual Merchants: Religion, Magic, and Commerce* (Knoxville, TN: University of Tennessee Press, 2001).

26. J. Lorand Matory, *Black Atlantic Religion: Tradition, Transnationalism, and Matriarchy in the Afro-Brazilian Candomblé* (Princeton, NJ: Princeton University Press, 2005), 3.

27. Raul Canizares, *Walking with the Night: The Afro-Cuban World of Santería* (Rochester, VT: Destiny Books, 1993); Michael Atwood Mason, *Living Santería: Rituals and Experiences in an Afro-Cuban Religion* (Washington, DC: Smithsonian Books, 2002).

28. As Afro-Caribbean scholar George Brandon points out in his monograph on Santería, "Some of the things I uncovered through the historical study and field research I had done threw much of what I had learned to accept as anthropological theory into question." George Brandon, *Santería from Africa to the New World: The Dead Sell Memories* (Bloomington: Indiana University Press, 1993), ix.

29. Stephan Palmié, *Wizards and Scientists: Explorations in Afro-Cuban Modernity and Tradition* (Durham, NC: Duke University Press, 2002), 14. The methodology of this book is historiography.

30. Joseph M. Murphy and Mei-Mei Sanford, eds., *Òsun across the Waters: A Yoruba Goddess in Africa and the Americas* (Bloomington: Indiana University Press, 2001).

31. See Johan Wedel, *Santería Healing: A Journey into the Afro-Cuban World of Divinities, Spirits, and Sorcery* (Gainesville: University Press of Florida, 2004).

32. The group's research focuses on uncovering the complexity of the Afro-Cuban religious landscape in Oriente; it highlights practices such as Muertéra Bembé de Sao, Palo Monte, Vodou in Cuba, and Espiritismo. See Jualynne E. Dodson, "African Descendent Women and Religion: Diaspora in Oriente Cuba," in *Women and New and Africana Religions*, ed. Lillian Ashcraft-Eason, Darnise C. Martin, and Oyeronke Olademo (Santa Barbara, CA: Praeger, 2010), 167–190, and Jualynne E. Dodson, *Sacred Spaces and Religious Traditions in Oriente Cuba* (Albuquerque: University of New Mexico Press, 2008).

33. Ivor L. Miller, *Voices of the Leopard: African Secret Societies and Cuba* (Jackson: University Press of Mississippi, 2009).

34. David H. Brown, *The Light Inside: Abakuá Society Arts and Cuban Cultural History* (Washington, DC: Smithsonian Institution Press, 2003), 4.

35. David H. Brown, *Santería Enthroned: Art, Ritual, and Innovation in an Afro-Cuban Religion* (Chicago: University of Chicago Press, 2003).

36. Ibid., 15.

37. Lindsay, *Santería Aesthetics*.

38. See Katherine J. Hagedorn, *Divine Utterances: The Performance of Afro-Cuban Santería* (Washington, DC: Smithsonian Institution Press, 2001), and Eugenio Matibag, *Afro-Cuban Religious Experience: Cultural Reflections in Narrative* (Gainesville: University Press of Florida, 1996).

39. "As literary texts reveal, the deities populate the religious subtexts of mythical story telling and divination rituals, which maintain their own archive of narrative knowledge." Matibag, *Afro-Cuban Religious Experience*, xiii.
40. Ibid., 26.
41. Stewart, "Womanist God-Talk," 79–80.
42. Ibid., 80.
43. Dianne M. Stewart, "Womanist Theology in the Caribbean Context: Critiquing Culture, Rethinking Doctrine, and Expanding Boundaries," in *Journal of Feminist Studies in Religion* 20:1 (Spring 2004), 61.
44. Mena López, "Globalisation and Gender Inequality," 159–160.
45. Deborah O'Neil and Terry Rey, "The Saint and the Siren: Liberation Hagiography in a Haitian Village," *Studies in Religion* 41:2 (2012): 170.
46. Terry Rey, *Our Lady of Class Struggle: The Cult of the Virgin Mary in Haiti* (Trenton, NJ: Africa World Press, 1999).
47. Terry Rey, "The Politics of Patron Sainthood in Haiti: 500 Years of Iconic Struggle," *Catholic Historical Review* 88:3 (July 2002), 521.

NOTES FOR THE CONCLUSION

1. In her 2011 presidential address to the American Academy of Religion, Kwok Pui Lan outlined three challenges for the present and in preparation for the future religious landscape. First, the field must undergo a paradigm shift in light of the changing racial demographics of the world. Second, Kwok called us to become more global as scholars and to move beyond the predominance of European and Euro-American scholarship. She concluded by discussing the harsh reality of the current economic context and its impact on our field. Instead of being mere curators of religion, we need to be public advocates for the significance of religion. Kwok Pui Lan, "2011 Presidential Address: Empire and the Study of Religion," *Journal of the American Academy of Religion* 80:2 (June 2012), 289–295.
2. In his introduction to his edited volume *The Hope of Liberation in World Religions*, Miguel De La Torre, describing the manner in which the marginalized turn to their religious traditions as a source of liberation and hope, argues that within world religions one can find kindred spirits in the struggle for liberation. Miguel A. De La Torre, "Introduction," in *The Hope of Liberation in World Religions*, ed. Miguel A. De La Torre (Waco, TX: Baylor University Press, 2008), 10.
3. Dianne M. Stewart, "Orisha Traditions in the West," in De La Torre, *The Hope of Liberation*, 245–246.
4. "Relatorio de la Consulta: Culturas y religions del negro en América en relacion con la teología de liberación," in *Cultura negra y teología*, ed. Quince Duncan et al. (San Jose, Costa Rica: Editorial DEI, 1996), 35. See, for example, the work of SOTER (Sociedade de Teologia e Ciêncas da Religião) and the World Forum on Theology and Liberation.

5. Diego Irarrázaval, "Salvación indígena y afroamericana," in *Along the Many Paths of God*, vol. 4, *Intercontinental Liberation Theology of Religious Pluralism,* ed. José María Vigil, Luiza E. Tomita, and Marcelo Barros (n.p.: Ecumenical Association of Third World Theologians, 2010), 51, http://tiempoaxial.org/AlongTheMany-Paths/EATWOT-AlongTheManyPathsIV-Bilingual.pdf.

6. Theologian Afonso Soares describes this syncretic faith in contrast to inculturated faith; syncretic faith sees absolute truth as being embodied in Christianity, which must be communicated in its local context. "When I say syncretic faith I emphasize that the breath of the Spirit is already in operation before-hand in the other cultural traditions, against or even despite contact with Christian communities." Soares challenges Roman Catholic theologians to explore the possibility of catholicity outside the Roman Catholic Church. Afonso Soares, "Syncretism: Theological Significance in a Pluralistic-Theology Perspective," in ibid., 88.

7. Orlando O. Espín, "Contours of a Latino/a Theology of Religions: In Dialogue with the Lukumí Religions," in *Grace and Humanness: Theological Reflections because of Culture*, ed. Orlando O. Espín (Maryknoll, NY: Orbis Books, 2007), 82.

8. Maricel Mena López, "Globalization and Gender Inequality: A Contribution from a Latino Afro-Feminist Perspective," in *The Oxford Handbook of Feminist Theology*, ed. Mary McClintock Fulkerson and Sheila Briggs (New York: Oxford University Press, 2012), 174.

9. Clara Luz Ajo Lázaro , "Jesus and Mary Dance with the *Orishas*," in *Feminist Intercultural Theology: Latina Explorations for a Just World*, ed. María Pilar Aquino and María José Rosado-Nunes (Maryknoll, NY: Orbis Books, 2007), 122.

10. María Pilar Aquino, "Theology and Identity in the Context of Globalization," in Mena López, *The Oxford Handbook of Feminist Theology*, 420.

11. Ivor L. Miller, *Voices of the Leopard: African Secret Societies and Cuba* (Jackson: University of Mississippi Press, 2009), 175.

12. Within Latino/a theology, sociologist Otto Maduro is critical of the "Christian sectarianism" that characterizes many approaches to popular religion. Religion is identified exclusively with Christianity and usually by denominational affiliation, leaving non-Christian religions as at best secondary and at worst abhorrent. "In this perspective, the living presence of native American and African religions in the Americas—as well as the existence of *mestizo, mulato,* and other 'syncretistic' religions, alongside with dynamic phenomena of plural religious belonging in significant segments of the Latino/a population—are discounted as negligible, secondary realities; or, at worst, as fictitious or abhorrent anomalies." Otto A. Maduro, "Directions of a Reassessment of Latina/o Religion," in Anthony M. Stevens-Arroyo and Andrés Pérez y Mena, eds., *Enigmatic Powers: Syncretism with African and Indigenous Peoples' Religions among Latinos* (New York: Program for the Analysis of Religion among Latinos, 1995), 57.

13. Brian Bantum, *Redeeming Mulatto: A Theology of Race and Christian Hybridity* (Waco, TX: Baylor University Press, 2010), 7.

14. Ibid., 99.

15. R. Andrew Chestnut, *Devoted to Death: Santa Muerte, the Skeleton Saint* (New York: Oxford University Press, 2012).

16. Marcella María Althaus-Reid, "Doing a Theology from Disappeared Bodies: Theology, Sexuality, and the Excluded Bodies of the Discourses of Latin American Liberation Theology," in Fulkerson and Briggs, *The Oxford Handbook of Feminist Theology*, 445.

17. Mary Ann Clark, *Where Men Are Wives and Mothers Rule: Santería Ritual Practices and Their Gender Implications* (Gainesville: University of Florida Press, 2005), 144.

18. "The religion scholar caught in the textualist attitude acts as the authorized interpreter of texts and the endless discourses on them, or of the deepest feelings and beliefs of the faithful. S/he becomes the sovereign master of a discursive field that is not conditioned by historical processes of othering." Manuel A. Vásquez, *More Than Belief: A Materialist Theory of Religion* (New York: Oxford University Press, 2011), 228.

19. James H. Evans, *We Have Been Believers: An African American Systematic Theology*, 2nd ed. (Minneapolis: Fortress Press, 2012), 2.

20. As noted by feminist theologian Elina Vuola regarding her own theological methodology, "Instead of using philosophy or social sciences, I construct my multi-disciplinary feminist theology in dialogue with disciplines such as anthropology and comparative folkloricists. . . . I also think that feminist theology could [be] working [in] much closer contact with scholars who study religion as 'lived religion,' without excluding the level of the symbolic." Elina Vuola, "*La Morenita* on Skis: Women's Popular Marian Piety and Feminist Research on Religion," in Fulkerson and Briggs, *The Oxford Handbook of Feminist Theology*, 495.

21. Nancy Pineda-Madrid, *Suffering and Salvation in Ciudad Juárez* (Minneapolis: Fortress Press, 2011).

22. Manuel A. Vásquez and Marie Friedmann Marquardt, *Globalizing the Sacred: Religion across the Americas* (New Brunswick, NJ: Rutgers University Press, 2003), 8.

23. Vásquez, *More Than Belief*, 15.

24. Ivan Petrella, "Introduction," in *Latin American Liberation Theology: The Next Generation*, ed. Ivan Petrella (Maryknoll, NY: Orbis Books, 2005), xiii.

25. Juan José Tamayo, *La teología de la liberación en el nuevo escenario político y religioso* (Valencia: Tirant Lo Blanch, 2009), 22–24.

26. "African Americans heard, read, and retold the story of the Exodus more than any other biblical narrative. In it they saw their own aspirations for liberation from bondage in the story of the ancient Hebrew slaves. The Exodus was the Bible's narrative argument that God was opposed to American slavery and would return catastrophic judgment against the nation as he had against ancient Egypt." Allen Dwight Callahan, *The Talking Book: African Americans and the Bible* (New

Haven, CT: Yale University Press, 2006), 83. For a study of the manner in which the Exodus story shapes language among African Americans, see Eddie S. Glaude, *Exodus! Religion, Race, and Nation in Early Nineteenth-Century Black America* (Chicago: University of Chicago Press, 2000).

27. Hector Avalos, *Slavery, Abolitionism, and the Ethics of Biblical Scholarship* (Sheffield, UK: Sheffield Phoenix Press, 2011), 74.

28. Jennifer A. Glancy, *Slavery in Early Christianity* (New York: Oxford University Press, 2002).

29. Francisco Lozada, "Reinventing the Biblical Tradition: An Exploration of Social Location Hermeneutics," in *Futuring Our Past: Explorations in the Theology of Tradition*, ed. Orlando O. Espín and Gary Macy (Maryknoll, NY: Orbis Books, 2006), 134.

30. Ibid., 114.

31. Adding a critical analysis to this insight, Maduro says, "At the risk of upsetting some people, I assume that we have the ethical responsibility to, every so often, pause and reflect humbly on the probable loss of sight, avoidances, and neglects that inevitably arise from any particular standpoint—including the standpoint of LALT (Latin American liberation theology)." Otto Maduro, "Once Again Liberating Theology? Towards a Latin American Liberation Theological Self-Criticism," in ibid., 21.

32. Jung Mo Sung, "The Human Being as Subject: Defending the Victims," in Petrella, *Latin American Liberation Theology*, 11.

33. Anthropologist Elizabeth McAlister traces the origins of this revisionist Christian history to the Spiritual Mapping evangelical movement in Haiti. Elizabeth McAlister, "From Slave Revolt to a Blood Pact with Satan: The Evangelical Rewriting of Haitian History," *Studies in Religion* 41:2 (2012), 187–215.

34. Stephan Palmié, *Explorations in Afro-Cuban Modernity and Tradition* (Durham, NC: Duke University Press, 2002), 27.

35. Argentinian liberation theologian Ivan Petrella appeals for U.S. liberation theologies to take the Americas as a whole seriously. "If U.S. liberation theologies do not place their claims for justice in the wider American context, then it seems that they are upset only because they have not been given a larger piece of the United States' pie. . . . Here a theology for the Americas must follow Latin American liberation theology's epistemological break from modern theology; that is, it must move theology away from the perspective of a small and affluent minority toward the perspective of the majority of humankind." Ivan Petrella, "Globalising Liberation Theology: The American Context, and Coda," in *The Cambridge Companion to Liberation Theology*, 2nd ed., ed. Christopher Rowland (New York: Cambridge University Press, 2007), 290.

36. "An intercultural epistemology requires that we move beyond mere recognition of differences toward designing common spaces for affirming the common emancipative interests of the voices that the dominant culture wishes to suppress."

Maricel Mena-López and María Pilar Aquino, "Feminist Intercultural Theology: Religion, Culture, Feminism, and Power," in Aquino and Rosado-Nunes, *Feminist Intercultural Theology*, xxv.

37. Ann Taves, "2010 Presidential Address: 'Religion' in the Humanities and Humanities in the University," *Journal of the American Academy of Religion* 79:2 (June 2011), 295.

# BIBLIOGRAPHY

Ajo Lázaro, Clara Luz. "Jesus and Mary Dance with the *Orishas*." In *Feminist Intercultural Theology: Latina Explorations for a Just World*. Edited by María Pilar Aquino and María José Rosado-Nunes, 109–124. Maryknoll, NY: Orbis Books, 2007.

Althaus-Reid, Marcella María. "Doing a Theology from Disappeared Bodies: Theology, Sexuality, and the Excluded Bodies of the Discourses of Latin American Liberation Theology." In *The Oxford Handbook of Feminist Theology*. Edited by Mary McClintock Fulkerson and Sheila Briggs, 441–455. New York: Oxford University Press, 2012.

———. "Gustavo Gutiérrez Goes to Disneyland: Theme Park Theologies and the Diaspora of the Discourse of the Popular Theologian in Liberation Theology." In *Interpreting Beyond Borders*. Edited by Fernando F. Segovia, 36–58. Sheffield, UK: Sheffield Academic Press, 2000.

———. *Indecent Theology: Theological Perversions in Sex, Gender and Politics*. London and New York: Routledge, 2000.

———, ed. *Liberation Theology and Sexuality*, 2nd ed. Burlington, VT: Ashgate, 2009.

Althaus-Reid, Marcella María, Ivan Petrella, and Luiz Carlos Susin, eds. *Another Possible World: Reclaiming Liberation Theology*. London: SCM Press, 2007.

Alvarez, Carmelo E. "Is Liberation Theology Finished?" *Encounter* 59:1–2 (1998): 197–208.

Ammerman, Nancy T., ed. *Everyday Religion: Observing Modern Religious Lives*. New York: Oxford University Press, 2007.

Anderson, Victor. *Beyond Ontological Blackness: An Essay on African American Religious and Cultural Criticism*. New York: Continuum, 1995.

———. *Creative Exchange: A Constructive Theology of African American Religious Experience*. Minneapolis: Fortress Press, 2009.

Aquino, María Pilar. *Our Cry for Life: Feminist Theology from Latin America*. Maryknoll, NY: Orbis Books, 1993.

———. "Theology and Identity in the Context of Globalization." In *The Oxford Handbook of Feminist Theology*. Edited by Mary McClintock Fulkerson and Sheila Briggs, 418–440. New York: Oxford University Press, 2012.

Atwood Mason, Michael. *Living Santería: Rituals and Experiences in an Afro-Cuban Religion*. Washington, D.C.: Smithsonian Books, 2002.

Badillo, David . *Latino/as and the New Immigrant Church*. Baltimore: Johns Hopkins University Press, 2006.

Baker-Fletcher, Karen. "Passing on the Spark: A Womanist Perspective on Theology and Culture." In *Changing Conversations: Religious Reflection and Cultural Analysis*. Edited by Dwight N. Hopkins and Sheila Greeve Davaney, 145–162. New York: Routledge, 1996.

Bantum, Brian. *Redeeming Mulatto: A Theology of Race and Christian Hybridity*. Waco, TX: Baylor University Press, 2010.

Batstone, David, Eduardo Mendieta, Lois Ann Lorentzen, and Dwight N. Hopkins, eds. *Liberation Theologies, Postmodernity, and the Americas*. New York: Routledge, 1991.

Bell, Daniel M., Jr. *Liberation Theology after the End of History: The Refusal to Cease Suffering*. New York: Routledge, 2001.

Boff, Leonardo. *Church: Charism and Power: Liberation Theology and the Institutional Church*. New York: Crossroad, 1985.

———. *Ecclesiogenesis: The Base Communities Reinvent the Church*. Maryknoll, NY: Orbis Books, 1986.

Boff, Leonardo, and Clodovis Boff. *Introducing Liberation Theology*. Maryknoll, NY: Orbis Books, 2001.

Brandon, George. *Santería from Africa to the New World: The Dead Sell Memories*. Bloomington: Indiana University Press, 1993.

Brown, Daniel H. "Altared Spaces: Afro-Cuban Religions and the Urban Landscape in Cuba and the United Sates." In *Gods of the City: Religion and the American Urban Landscape*. Edited by Robert A. Orsi, 155–230. Bloomington: Indiana University Press, 1999.

———. *The Light Inside: Abakuá Society Arts and Cuban Cultural History*. Washington, DC: Smithsonian Institution Press, 2003.

———. *Santería Enthroned: Art, Ritual, and Innovation in an Afro-Cuban Religion*. Chicago: University of Chicago Press, 2003.

Butler, Anthea D. *Women in the Church of God in Christ: Making a Sanctified World*. Chapel Hill: The University of North Carolina Press, 2007.

Candelaria, Michael R. *Popular Religion and Liberation: The Dilemma of Liberation Theology*. Albany: State University Press of New York, 1990.

Canizares, Raul. *Walking with the Night: The Afro-Cuban World of Santería*. Rochester, VT: Destiny Books, 1993.

Carter, J. Kameron. *Race: A Theological Account*. New York: Oxford University Press, 2008.

CELAM. "Medellín Conclusiones: La Iglesia en la actual transformación de América Latina a la Luz del Concilio." In *Segunda conferencia general del Episcopado Latinoamericano.* Edited by Episcopado Latinoamericano. Medellín, Colombia: Consejo Episcopal Latino Americano, 1968.

Chesnut, R. Andrew. *Devoted to Death: Santa Muerte, the Skeleton Saint.* New York: Oxford University Press, 2012.

———. "A Preferential Option for the Spirit: The Catholic Charismatic Renewal in Latin America's New Religious Economy," *Latin American Politics and Society* 45:1 (Spring 2003): 55–85.

Chopp, Rebecca S. "Beyond the Founding Fratricidal Conflict: A Tale of Three Cities," *Journal of the American Academy of Religion* 70:3 (2002): 461–474.

Clark, Jwanza Eric. *Indigenous Black Theology: Toward an African-Centered Theology of the African-American Religious Experience.* Gordonsville, PA: Palgrave Macmillan, 2012.

Clark, Mary Ann. *Where Men Are Wives and Mothers Rule: Santería Ritual Practices and Their Gender Implications.* Gainesville: University Press of Florida, 2005.

Clarke, Kamari Maxine. *Mapping Yorùbá Networks: Power and Agency in the Making of Transnational Communities.* Durham, NC: Duke University Press, 2004.

Cleary, Edward L. *Crisis and Change: The Church in Latin America Today.* Maryknoll, NY: Orbis Books, 1985.

———. *The Rise of Charismatic Catholicism in Latin America.* Gainesville: University Press of Florida, 2011.

Coleman, Monica. *Making a Way Out of No Way: A Womanist Theology.* Minneapolis: Fortress Press, 2008.

Comblin, José. *Called for Freedom: The Changing Context of Liberation Theology.* Maryknoll, NY: Orbis Books, 1998.

Cone, James H. *God of the Oppressed.* San Francisco: Harper San Francisco, 1975.

Cros Sandoval, Mercedes. *Worldview, the Orichas, and Santería: Africa to Cuba and Beyond.* Gainesville: University Press of Florida, 2006.

Daudelin, Jean, and W. E. Hewitt. "Latin American Politics: Exit the Catholic Church?" In *Organized Religion in the Political Transformation of Latin American.* Edited by Satya R. Pattnayak, 177–194. (Lanham, MD: University Press of America, 1995).

De La Torre, Miguel A., ed. *The Hope of Liberation in World Religions.* Waco, TX: Baylor University Press, 2008.

De La Torre, Miguel A., and Edwin David Aponte, eds. *Handbook of Latino/a Theologies.* St. Louis, MO: Chalice Press, 2006.

———. *Introducing Latino/a Theologies.* Maryknoll, NY: Orbis Books, 2001.

De La Torre, Miguel A., and Gastón Espinosa, eds. *Rethinking Latino(a) Religion and Identity.* Cleveland, OH: Pilgrim Press, 2006.

De Lima Silva, Silvia Regina. "Dialogue of Memories: Ways toward a Black Feminist Christology from Latin America." In *Feminist Intercultural Theology: Latina*

*Explorations for a Just World.* Edited by María Pilar Aquino and María José Rosado-Nunes, 166–178. Maryknoll, NY: Orbis Books, 2007.

Deloria, Vine. *For This Land: Writings on Religion in America.* New York: Routledge, 2000.

Desmangles, Leslie G., Stephen D. Glazier, and Joseph M. Murphy. "Religion in the Caribbean." In *Understanding the Contemporary Caribbean.* Edited by Richard S. Hillman and Thomas J. D'Agostino, 263–304. Boulder: Lynne Rienner, 2003.

de Theije, Marjo. "Charismatic Renewal and Base Communities: The Religious Participation of Women in a Brazilian Parish." In *More Than Opium: An Anthropological Approach to Latin American and Caribbean Pentecostal Practice.* Edited by Barbara Boudewijnse, A. F. Droogers, and Frans Kamsteeg, 225–248. Lanham, MD: Scarecrow Press, 1998.

Dodson, Jualynne E. "African Descendent Women and Religion: Diaspora in Oriente Cuba." In *Women and New and Africana Religions.* Edited by Lillian Ashcraft-Eason, Darnise C. Martin, and Oyeronke Olademo, 167–190. Santa Barbara, CA: Praeger, 2010.

———. *Sacred Spaces and Religious Traditions in Oriente Cuba.* Albuquerque, NM: University of New Mexico Press, 2008.

Duncan, Quince, et al. *Cultura negra y teología.* San Jose, Costa Rica: Editorial DEI, 1996.

Dyson, Michael Eric. *The Michael Eric Dyson Reader.* New York: Basic Civitas Books, 2004.

Elizondo, Virgilio. "*Mestizaje* as a Locus for Theological Reflection." In *Frontiers of Hispanic Theology in the United States.* Edited by Allan Figueroa Deck, 104–123. Maryknoll, NY: Orbis Books, 1992.

Ellacuría, Ignacio, and Jon Sobrino, eds. *Mysterium Liberationis: Fundamental Concepts of Liberation Theology.* Maryknoll, NY: Orbis Books, 1993.

Espín, Orlando O. *Building Bridges, Doing Justice: Constructing a Latino/a Ecumenical Theology.* Maryknoll, NY: Orbis Books, 2009.

———. *Grace and Humanness: Theological Reflections because of Culture.* Maryknoll, NY: Orbis Books, 2007.

———. "Traditioning: Culture, Daily Life, and Popular Religion, and Their Impact on the Christian Tradition." In *Futuring Our Past: Explorations in the Theology of Tradition.* Edited by Orlando O. Espín and Gary Macy, 1–22. Maryknoll, NY: Orbis Books, 2006.

Espín, Orlando O., and Miguel H. Díaz, eds. *From the Heart of Our People: Latino/a Explorations in Systematic Theology.* Maryknoll, NY: Orbis Books, 1999.

Espinosa, Gastón, Virgilio Elizondo, and Jesse Miranda, eds. *Latino Religions and Civic Activism in the United States.* New York: Oxford University Press, 2005.

Espinosa, Gastón, and Mario T. García, eds. *Mexican American Religions: Spirituality, Activism, and Culture.* Durham, NC: Duke University Press, 2008.

Espirito Santo, Diana. "The Power of the Dead: Spirits, Socialism, and Selves in an Afro-Cuban Universe." *Fieldwork in Religion* 3:2 (2008): 161–177.

Evans, James H. *We Have Been Believers: An African American Systematic Theology*, 2nd ed. Minneapolis: Fortress Press, 2012.

Fernández, Eduardo C. *Mexican-American Catholics*. New York: Paulist Press, 2007.

Fernández Olmos, Margarite, and Lizabeth Paravisini-Gebert, eds. *Sacred Possessions: Vodou, Santería, Obeah and the Caribbean*. New Brunswick, NJ: Rutgers University Press, 2007.

Floyd Thomas, Stacey M., and Anthony B. Pinn, eds. *Liberation Theologies in the United States: An Introduction*. New York: New York University Press, 2010.

Frederick, Marla F. *Between Sundays: Black Women and Everyday Struggles of Faith*. Berkeley; University of California Press, 2003.

Gibellini, Rosini. *The Liberation Theology Debate*. Maryknoll, NY: Orbis Books, 1987.

Goldschmidt, Henry, and Elizabeth McAlister, eds. *Race, Nation, and Religion in the Americas*. New York: Oxford University Press, 2004.

Gonzalez, Michelle A. *Afro-Cuban Theology: Religion, Race, Culture, and Identity*. Gainesville: University Press of Florida, 2006.

Graziano, Frank. *Cultures of Devotion: Folk Saints of Spanish America*. New York: Oxford University Press, 2007.

Greinacher, Norbert, and Norbert Mette, eds. *Popular Religion*. Edinburgh: T & T Clark, 1986.

Gutiérrez, Gustavo. *A Theology of Liberation*. 15th anniversary ed. Maryknoll, NY: Orbis Books, 1988.

———. *We Drink from Our Own Wells: The Spiritual Journey of People*. Maryknoll, NY: Orbis Books, 2003.

Hagedorn, Katherine J. *Divine Utterances: The Performance of Afro-Cuban Santería*. Washington: Smithsonian Institution Press, 2001.

Hall, David D., ed. *Lived Religion in America: Toward a History of Practice*. Princeton, NJ: Princeton University Press, 1997.

Hart, D. G. *The University Gets Religion: Religious Studies in American Higher Education*. Baltimore, MD: Johns Hopkins University Press, 1999.

Hewitt, W. E. "From Defenders of the People to Defenders of the Faith: A 1984–1993 Retrospective of CEB Activity in São Paulo." *Latin American Perspectives* 25:1 (Jan. 1998): 170–191.

Holmes, Barbara A. *Race and the Cosmos*. Harrisburg, PA: Trinity Press International, 2002.

Hopkins, Dwight N., ed. *Black Faith and Public Talk: Critical Essays on James H. Cone's "Black Theology and Black Power."* Maryknoll, NY: Orbis Books, 1999.

———. *Black Theology of Liberation*. Maryknoll, NY: Orbis Books, 1999.

Hopkins, Dwight N., and Edward P. Antonio, eds. *The Cambridge Companion to Black Theology*. New York: Cambridge University Press, 2012.

Hopkins, Dwight N., and George C.L. Cummings, eds., *Cut Loose Your Stammering Tongue: Black Theology in the Slave Narrative*, 2nd ed. Louisville, KY: Westminster John Knox Press, 2003.

Hopkins, Dwight N., and Marjorie Lewis, eds. *Another World Is Possible: Spiritualities and Religions of Global Darker Peoples*. London: Equinox Pub, 2009.

Hurbon, Laënnec. "Globalization and the Evolution of Haitian Vodou." In *Òrìṣà Devotion As World Religion: The Globalization of Yorùbá Religious Culture*. Edited by Jacob K. Olupona and Terry Rey, 263–277. Madison: University of Wisconsin Press, 2008.

Irvine, Andrew B. "Liberation Theology in Late Modernity: An Argument for a Symbolic Approach," *Journal of the American Academy of Religion* 78:4 (Dec. 2010): 921–960.

Isasi-Díaz, Ada María. *En la Lucha / In the Struggle: Elaborating a Mujerista Theology*. Minneapolis: Fortress Press, 1993.

Johnson, Elizabeth A. *The Quest for the Living God: Mapping Frontiers in the Theology of God*. New York: Continuum, 2007.

Jones, William R. *Is God a White Racist? A Preamble to Black Theology*. Boston: Beacon Press, 1997.

Kee, Alistair. *The Rise and Demise of Black Theology*. London: SCM Press, 2008.

Kudó, Tokihiro. *Práctica religiosa y proyecto histórico: Estudio sobre la religiosidad popular en dos barrios en Lima*. Lima, Peru: CEP, 1980.

Lee, Michael E. "A Way Forward for Latino/a Christology." In *In Our Own Voices: Latino/a Renditions of Theology*. Edited by Benjamín Valentín, 112–132. Maryknoll, NY: Orbis Books, 2010.

León, Luis D. *La Llorona's Children: Religion, Life, and Death in the U.S.-Mexican Borderlands*. Berkeley: University of California Press, 2004.

Levine, Daniel H. *Popular Voices in Latin American Catholicism*. Princeton, NJ: Princeton University Press, 1992.

———, ed. *Religion and Political Conflict in Latin America*. Chapel Hill: University of North Carolina Press, 1986.

Lindsay, Arturo, ed. *Santería Aesthetics in Contemporary Latin American Art*. Washington, DC: Smithsonian Institution Press, 1996.

Long, Carolyn Morrow. *Spiritual Merchants: Religion, Magic, and Commerce*. Knoxville: University of Tennessee Press, 2001.

Löwy, Michael. *The War of Gods: Religion and Politics in Latin America*. New York: Verso, 1996.

Maduro, Otto A. "Directions of a Reassessment of Latina/o Religion." In *Enigmatic Powers: Syncretism with African and Indigenous Peoples' Religions among Latinos*, Vol. 3. Edited by Anthony M. Stevens-Arroyo and Andrés Pérez y Mena, 47–68. New York: PARAL, 1995.

Martinez, Gaspar. *Confronting the Mystery of God: Political, Liberation, and Public Theologies*. New York: Continuum, 2001.

Massingale, Bryan N. *Racial Justice and the Catholic Church*. Maryknoll, NY: Orbis Books, 2010.

Matibag, Eugenio. *Afro-Cuban Religious Experience: Cultural Reflections in Narrative.* Gainesville: University Press of Florida, 1996.

Matory, J. Lorand. *Black Atlantic Religion: Tradition, Transnationalism, and Matriarchy in the Afro-Brazilian Candomblé.* Princeton, NJ: Princeton University Press, 2005.

Matovina, Timothy M., ed. *Beyond Borders: Writings of Virgilio Elizondo and Friends.* Maryknoll, NY: Orbis Books, 2000.

———. *Guadalupe and Her Faithful: Latino Catholics in San Antonio, from Colonial Origins to the Present.* Baltimore: Johns Hopkins University Press, 2005.

Matovina, Timothy M., and Gary Riebe-Estrella, eds. *Horizons of the Sacred: Mexican Traditions in U.S. Catholicism.* Ithaca, NY: Cornell University Press, 2002.

McAlister, Elizabeth. "From Slave Revolt to a Blood Pact with Satan: The Evangelical Rewriting of Haitian History," *Studies in Religion* 41:2 (2012): 187–215.

McCarthy Brown, Karen. *Mama Lola: A Vodou Priestess in Brooklyn.* Berkeley: University of California Press, 1991.

———. "Staying Grounded in a High-Rise Building: Ecological Dissonance and Ritual Accommodation in Haitian Vodou." In *Gods of the City: Religion and the American Urban Landscape.* Edited by Robert A. Orsi, 79–102. Bloomington: Indiana University Press, 1999.

McFarland Taylor, Sarah. *Green Sisters: A Spiritual Ecology.* Cambridge, MA: Harvard University Press, 2007.

McGuire, Meredith B. *Lived Religion: Faith and Practice in Everyday Life.* New York: Oxford University Press, 2006.

Mejido, Manuel J. "The Fundamental Problematic of U.S. Hispanic Theology." In *New Horizons in Hispanic/Latino(a) Theology.* Edited by Benjamín Valentín, 164–180. Cleveland, OH: Pilgrim Press, 2003.

Mena López, Maricel. "Globalisation and Gender Inequality: A Contribution from a Latino Afro-Feminist Perspective." In *The Oxford Handbook of Feminist Theology.* Edited by Mary McClintock Fulkerson and Sheila Briggs, 157–179. New York: Oxford University Press, 2012.

Miles, Margaret R. "Becoming Answerable for What We See," *Journal of the American Academy of Religion* 68:3 (2000): 472–485.

Miller, Donald E. and Tetsunao Yamamori, eds. *Global Pentecostalism: The New Face of Christian Social Engagement.* Berkeley: University of California Press, 2007.

Miller, Ivor L. *Voices of the Leopard: African Secret Societies and Cuba.* Jackson: University Press of Mississippi, 2009.

Mitchem, Stephanie. *African American Folk Healing.* New York: New York University Press, 2007.

Murphy, Joseph M. *Santería: African Spirits in America.* Boston: Beacon Press, 1993.

Murphy, Joseph M., and Mei-Mei Sanford, eds. *Òsun across the Waters: A Yoruba Goddess in Africa and the Americas.* Bloomington: Indiana University Press, 2001.

Nabhan-Warren, Kristy. *The Virgin of El Barrio: Marian Apparitions, Catholic Evangelizing, and Mexican American Activism.* New York: New York University Press, 2005.

Ochoa, Todd Ramón. *Society of the Dead: Quita Manaquita and Palo Praise in Cuba.* Berkeley: University of California Press, 2010.

Olupona, Jacob K., and Terry Rey, eds. *Òrìṣà Devotion as World Religion: The Globalization of Yorùbá Religious Culture.* Madison: University of Wisconsin Press, 2008.

O'Neil, Deborah, and Terry Rey. "The Saint and the Siren: Liberation Hagiography in a Haitian Village," *Studies in Religion* 41:2 (2012): 166–186.

Orsi, Robert A. *Between Heaven and Earth: The Religious World People Make and the Scholars That Study Them.* Princeton, NJ: Princeton University Press, 2006.

———. *The Madonna of 115th Street: Faith and Community in Italian Harlem, 1880–1950,* 2nd ed. New Haven, CT: Yale University Press, 2002.

———. *Thank You St. Jude: Women's Devotion to the Patron Saint of Hopeless Causes.* New Haven, CT.: Yale University Press, 1996.

Ortiz, Fernando O., and Kenneth G. Davis, "Latino/a Folk Saints and Marian Devotions: Popular Religiosity and Healing." In *Latino/a Healing Practices: Mestizo and Indigenous Perspectives.* Edited by Brian W. McNeill and Joseph M. Cervantes, 29–62. New York: Routledge, 2009.

Palmié, Stephan. *Wizards and Scientists: Explorations in Afro-Cuban Modernity and Tradition.* Durham, NC: Duke University Press, 2002.

Peña, Milagros. "Liberation Theology in Peru: An Analysis of the Role of Intellectuals in Social Movements," *Journal for the Scientific Study of Religion* 33:1 (1994): 34–45.

Penyal, Lee M., and Walter J. Petry, eds. *Religion and Society in Latin America: Interpretive Essays from Conquest to Present.* Maryknoll, NY: Orbis Books, 2009.

Peterson, Anna L., and Manuel A. Vásquez, eds. *Latin American Religions: Histories and Documents in Context.* New York: New York University Press, 2008.

Peterson, Anna L., Manuel A. Vásquez, and Philip J. Williams, eds. *Christianity, Social Change, and Globalization in the Americas.* New Brunswick, NJ: Rutgers University Press, 2001.

Petrella, Ivan. *The Future of Liberation Theology: An Argument and Manifesto.* London: SCM Press, 2006.

———, ed. *Latin American Liberation Theology: The Next Generation.* Maryknoll, NY: Orbis Books, 2005.

Phan, Peter C. "Method in Liberation Theologies," *Theological Studies* 61 (2000): 40–63.

Pieris, Aloysius, S.J. *An Asian Theology of Liberation.* Edinburgh: T & T Clark, 1988.

Pineda-Madrid, Nancy. "Latina Feminist Theology." In *New Feminist Christianity: Many Voices, Many Views.* Edited by Mary E. Hunt and Diann L. Neu, 21–29. Woodstock, VT: Skylight Paths, 2010.

———. *Suffering and Salvation in Ciudad Juárez.* Minneapolis: Fortress Press, 2011.

Pinn, Anthony B. *Terror and Triumph: The Nature of Black Religion.* Minneapolis: Fortress Press, 2003.

———. *Varieties of African American Religious Experience.* Minneapolis: Fortress Press, 1998.

———. *Why Lord? Suffering and Evil in Black Theology.* New York: Continuum, 1995.

Pui Lan, Kwok. "2011 Presidential Address: Empire and the Study of Religion," *Journal of the American Academy of Religion* 80:2 (June 2012): 285–303.

Recinos, Harold J., ed. *Wading Through Many Voices: Toward a Theology of Public Conversation.* Lanham, MD: Rowman & Littlefield, 2011.

Recinos, Harold J., and Hugo Magallanes, eds. *Jesus in the Hispanic Community: Images of Christ from Theology to Popular Religion.* Louisville, KY: Westminster John Knox Press, 2009.

Reid, Michele. "The Yoruba in Cuba: Origins, Identities, and Transformations." In *The Yoruba Diaspora in the Atlantic World.* Edited by Toyin Falola and Matt D. Childs, 111–129. Bloomington: Indiana University Press, 2004.

Rey, Terry. *Our Lady of Class Struggle: The Cult of the Virgin Mary in Haiti.* Trenton, NJ: Africa World Press, 1999.

———. "The Politics of Patron Sainthood in Haiti: 500 Years of Iconic Struggle," *Catholic Historical Review* 88:3 (July 2002): 519–545.

Rieger, Joerg. *Christ and Empire: From Paul to Postcolonial Times.* Minneapolis: Fortress Press, 2007.

———, ed. *Opting for the Margins: Postmodernity and Liberation in Christian Theology.* New York: Oxford University Press, 2003.

Rosario Rodríguez, Ruben. *Racism and God-Talk: A Latino/a Perspective.* New York: New York University Press, 2008

Rowland, Christopher, ed. *The Cambridge Companion to Liberation Theology,* 2nd ed. New York: Cambridge University Press, 2007.

Savage, Barbara Dianne. *Your Spirits Walk Beside Us: The Politics of Black Religion.* Cambridge, MA: Harvard University Press, 2008.

Scheper Hughes, Jennifer. *Biography of a Mexican Crucifix: Lived Religion and Local Faith from the Conquest to the Present.* New York: Oxford University Press, 2010.

Segovia, Fernando F., and Eleazar S. Fernandez , eds. *A Dream Unfinished: Theological Reflections on America from the Margins.* Maryknoll, NY: Orbis Books, 2001

———. "Toward Latino/a American Biblical Criticism: Latino(a)ness as Problematic." In *They Were All Together in One Place? Toward Minority Biblical Criticism.* Edited by Randall C. Bailey, Tat-Siong Benny Liew, and Fernando F. Segovia, 193–226. Atlanta, GA: Society of Biblical Literature, 2009.

Sigmund, Paul E. *Liberation Theology at the Crossroads: Democracy or Revolution?* New York: Oxford University Press, 1990.

Smith, Christian. *The Emergence of Liberation Theology: Radical Religion and Social Movement Theory.* Chicago: University of Chicago Press, 1991.

Stewart, Dianne M. "Dancing Limbo: Black Passages through the Boundaries of Place, Race, Class, and Religion." In *Deeper Shades of Purple: Womanism in Religion and Society.* Edited by Stacey M. Floyd-Thomas, 82–97. New York: New York University Press, 2006.

———. "Womanist God-Talk on the Cutting Edge of Theology and Black Religious Studies: Assessing the Contribution of Delores Williams," *Union Seminary Quarterly Review,* 58:3–4 (Fall 2004): 59–77.

———. "Womanist Theology in the Caribbean Context: Critiquing Culture, Rethinking Doctrine, and Expanding Boundaries," *Journal of Feminist Studies in Religion* 20:1 (Spring 2004): 61–82.

Stoll, David. *Is Latin America Turning Protestant? The Politics of Evangelical Growth.* Berkeley: University of California Press, 1990.

———. *Tongues of Fire: The Explosion of Protestantism in Latin America.* Oxford, UK: Blackwell, 1990.

Taves, Ann. "2010 Presidential Address: 'Religion' in the Humanities and Humanities in the University," *Journal of the American Academy of Religion* 79:2 (June 2011): 287–314.

Thistlethwaite, Susan Brooks. "On Becoming a Traitor: The Academic Liberation Theologian and the Future." In *Liberating the Future: God, Mammon, and Theology.* Edited by Joerg Rieger, 14–26. Minneapolis: Fortress Press, 1998.

Torres, Sergio, and Virginia Fabella, eds. *The Emergent Gospel: Theology from the Underside of History.* Maryknoll, NY: Orbis Books, 1978.

Tweed, Thomas A. *Our Lady of the Exile: Diasporic Religion at a Cuban Catholic Shrine in Miami.* New York: Oxford University Press, 1997.

Valentín, Benjamín. "*Nuevos Odres para el Vino*: A Critical Contribution to Latino/a Theological Construction," *Journal of Hispanic/Latino Theology* 5:4 (1998): 30–47.

Vásquez, Manuel A. *More Than Belief: A Materialist Theory of Religion.* New York: Oxford University Press, 2011.

———. "Toward a New Agenda for the Study of Religion in the Americas," *Journal of Interamerican Studies and World Affairs* 41:4 (1999): 1–20.

Vásquez, Manuel A., and Marie Friedmann Marquardt. *Globalizing the Sacred: Religion across the Americas.* New Brunswick, NJ: Rutgers University Press, 2003.

Vuola, Elina. "*La Morenita* on Skis: Women's Popular Marian Piety and Feminist Research on Religion." In *The Oxford Handbook of Feminist Theology.* Edited by Mary McClintock Fulkerson and Sheila Briggs, 494–524. New York: Oxford University Press, 2012.

———. "Radical Eurocentrism: The Crisis and Death of Latin America Liberation Theology and Recipes for Its Improvement." In *Interpreting the Postmodern: Responses to "Radical Orthodoxy."* Edited by Rosemary Radford Ruether and Marion Grau, 57–75. New York: T & T Clark, 2006.

Wedel, Johan. *Santería Healing: A Journey into the Afro-Cuban World of Divinities, Spirits, and Sorcery.* Gainesville: University Press of Florida, 2004.

West, Cornel. *The Cornel West Reader*. New York: Civitas Books, 1999.

———. *Prophetic Fragments*. Grand Rapids, MI: Eerdman, 1988.

West, Cornel, and Eddie S. Glaude Jr., eds. *African American Religious Thought: An Anthology*. Louisville, KY: Westminster John Knox Press, 2003.

Wiebe, Donald. "An Eternal Return All Over Again: The Religious Conversation Endures," *Journal of the American Academy of Religion* 74:3 (2006): 674–696.

Wilmore, Gayraud S., ed. *African American Religious Studies: An Interdisciplinary Anthology*. Durham, NC: Duke University Press, 1989.

Witrz, Kristina. *Ritual, Discourse, and Community in Cuban Santería*. Gainesville: University Press of Florida, 2007.

# INDEX

AAR. *See* American Academy of Religion

Abakuá, 119, 132–33

Academic liberation theology, 25–26, 42

Academic roots: of black liberation theology, 52, 67–68; of Latin American liberation theology, 26–36; of Latino/a theology, 80, 85–86

Academy of Catholic Hispanic Theologians in the United States (ACHTUS), 80

Accountability, 21–22, 46, 61, 116; communities of, 86

ACHTUS. *See* Academy of Catholic Hispanic Theologians in the United States

Advocacy, 7, 10–12, 19, 142

Aesthetics, 119–20, 160n53, 160n55

African American Christianity, 52, 53, 55, 65, 67, 70, 72, 74, 122. *See also* Black Church

African American religion, 52, 53, 77; challenges, 64–65; diversity, 60–61, 65–66; dress and ornamentation in, 75–76; experiences, 55, 59; politics and, 57, 69–70. *See also* Black liberation theology; *specific religions*

African American religious studies, 5, 52, 53, 61, 63, 64, 69

*African American Religious Thought: An Anthology* (West & Glaude), 64

African Americans: Exodus narrative and, 51, 105, 106, 139, 140, 141, 166n26; folk healing, 60; meaning making, 74–75; polarization, 58–59; redemptive suffering and, 61–62, 70, 74–76

African diaspora religion, 6, 103; construction of poor and, 136; critiques of, 141–42; decentering Christianity, 104–7; as demonic, 132; identity and, 133–34;

interdisciplinary methodology of studies, 114–21; liberation theology linked to, 103–4, 121–25, 133–34; Roman Catholicism and, 107–8, 116, 119, 120–21; study of, 107–21. *See also* Santería; Vodou

African theology, 106–7

Afrocubanismo, 117

Afro-Cuban religion, 116, 117, 118, 119, 141–42, 162n20

Afro-Latin Americans, 110, 129

Althaus-Reid, Marcela, 19, 20, 41, 50, 136, 146n28; "indecent" theology, 45–46

Alvarez, Carmelo, 150n43

Alves, Rubem, 41

American Academy of Religion (AAR), 9, 128, 164n1

Ancestors, 72, 73

Anderson, Victor, 56–58, 89

Anthropology, 73, 75, 100, 103, 117–20, 134, 147n34, 152n58

*The Anthropology of Christianity* (Cannell), 147n34

Aponte, Edwin, 82, 87

*Apuntes* journal, 80

Aquino, Jorge, 100

Aquino, María Pilar, 44–45, 81, 167n36

ASETT. *See* La Asociación de Téologos del Tercer Mundo

*Ashé* force, 112–13

La Asociación de Téologos del Tercer Mundo (ASETT), 129

Association of Third World Theologians. *See* La Asociación de Téologos del Tercer Mundo

Authority, 8, 13–14, 22; ecclesial, 32, 34, 65

Authorship, 6, 18, 83–84, 100

15, 97; method of, 90–99; popular religion and, 15, 94–99, 100–101; public of, 84–87; Roman Catholicism and, 79, 80, 86, 90; subjects of, 87–90; today, 138–39
Lee, Michael, 90
León, Luis D., 92
Liberation hagiography, 123
Liberationist narrative, 106, 139
Liberation theology: academic, 25–26, 42; African diaspora religions and, 103–4, 121–25, 133–34; challenges, 1–2; complexity, 147n2; construction of poor, 136; decentering Christianity, 104–7; framing and defining, 3–7; identity and, 133–37; inroads of dialogue, 128–33; Latino/a theology question, 80–84, 101–2; levels, 25, 147n2; liberationist, 83; lived religion and, 14–18; marginalization and death of, 18–23, 25–26, 146n25, 150n40; Native American, 105–6; non-Christian religions and, 128–33; religion reconceived, 137–43; starting point, 22–23; today, 138–39. See also Black liberation theology; Interdisciplinary methodology; Latin American liberation theology; Latino/a theology
Lived religion, 14, 16–18, 138, 152n58; Latin American liberation theology and, 15, 42–45; Latino/a theology and, 15, 97
Loas (spirits), 108–10, 121
Local religion, 43–44, 98, 138
Long, Charles, 56, 61
Löwy, Michael, 149n31
Lucumí religion, 111, 162n14. See also Santería
Lynching tree, 74

Maduro, Otto, 37, 165n12, 167n31
Mahon, Leo, 28
Mama Lola: A Vodou Priestess in Brooklyn (McCarthy Brown), 115–16
Martell-Ortero, Loida, 82
Marxism, 12, 37, 38, 42
Massingale, Bryan, 63–64
Materialist phenomenology, 15
Matibag, Eugenio, 121
Matovina, Timothy, 93, 158n30
McAlister, Elizabeth, 45, 167n33
McCarthy Brown, Karen, 115, 116
McFarland Taylor, Sarah, 15–16
McGuire, Meredith, 97
Mediocrity, 67
Mena López, Maricel, 123, 131, 167n36

Method, 127; of Latino/a theology, 90–99; liberationist, 82–83; theocentrism versus, 48–50. See also Interdisciplinary methodology
Mexican American Cultural Center, 85
Miles, Margaret, 9, 11, 12–13
Miller, Ivor, 132–33
Modernization, 44
Morrow Long, Carolyn, 115
Movimiento evangélicos. See Evangélicos movement
Mujerista, 82, 156n3
Murphy, Joseph, 115
Mythology, 120

Nabhan-Warren, Kristy, 93–94, 99, 101
National Committee of Black Churchmen, Statement July 31, 1966, 52
National Conference of Brazilian Bishops (CNBB), 35
Native American liberation theology, 105–6
"New Christendom" project, 35
Non-Christian religions, 48, 86–87, 127–28; black liberation theology and, 59, 72–74; Christianity and, 104–5, 110, 135–36, 140–42, 165n12; liberation in, 128–33; racism and, 128. See also African diaspora religion; specific religions
Nonpersons, 25
Nouvelle Théologie, 35

Obama, Barack, 69
Objectivity, 9–10
Olodumare, 112
Olofi, 112
Olorun, 112
O'Neil, Deborah, 123
Oppression, 18; blackness and, 54–55; faith experience and, 1; God and, 48–49, 61–62, 66; oversimplification of, 140; shared experience of, 21, 147n32
Orishas (spirits), 111–14, 115, 118, 121, 134, 162n16
Orsi, Robert, 15, 97, 159n44
Ortiz, Fernando, 117
Oshun, 118, 134
Our Cry for Life: Feminist Theology from Latin America (Aquino), 44
Our Lady of Charity, 93
Our Lady of Guadalupe, 93
Outsider, 7, 14, 16, 89, 92, 143

Michelle A. Gonzalez (Michelle Gonzalez Maldonado) is Associate Professor of Religious Studies at the University of Miami. Her research and teaching interests include Latino/a, Latin American, and feminist theologies, and she does interdisciplinary work in Afro-Caribbean Studies as well.